The Patterns of Social Behavior series
Zick Rubin, *Harvard University, General Editor*

This series brings both psychological and sociological perspectives to bear on the ways in which people affect one another. Each volume explores research on a particular aspect of social behavior and considers its personal and social implications.

VALERIAN J. DERLEGA and ALAN L. CHAIKIN, both social psychologists, are on the faculty of the Department of Psychology at Old Dominion University, Norfolk, Virginia, where Dr. Derlega is also director of the Psychology Graduate Program. Both authors are Woodrow Wilson Fellows. They are co-authors of *Self-Disclosure* (a module for General Learning Press), and numerous articles on intimacy in social relationships.

sharing intimacy

what we reveal to others and why

VALERIAN J. DERLEGA

ALAN L. CHAIKIN

A SPECTRUM BOOK

prentice-hall, inc., englewood cliffs, new jersey

Library of Congress Cataloging in Publication Data

DERLEGA, VALERIAN J

Sharing intimacy.

(A Spectrum Book)
Includes bibliographical references and index.
1. Interpersonal relations. 2. Intimacy
(Psychology) 3. Self-perception. I. Chaikin,
Alan L., joint author. II. Title.
HM132.D47   158'.2   75–9865
ISBN 0–13–807867–X
ISBN 0–13–807859–9 pbk.

10   9   8   7   6   5   4   3   2   1

PRENTICE-HALL INTERNATIONAL, INC. (*London*)
PRENTICE-HALL OF AUSTRALIA PTY., LTD. (*Sydney*)
PRENTICE-Hall of CANDADA, LTD. (*Toronto*)
PRENTICE-HALL OF INDIA PRIVATE LIMITED (*New Delhi*)
PRENTICE-HALL OF JAPAN, INC. (*Tokyo*)
PRENTICE-HALL OF SOUTHEAST ASIA (PTE.) LTD. (*Singapore*)

For our sons,
JOHN *and* ERIK

contents

preface

How do we become close to others? In friendship, marriage, psychotherapy, and even in a commune, individuals confront this question. American society is in flux: people change addresses and jobs faster than the Census Bureau can count; friendships that survive more than a few months or years are unusual; and the number of intimate confidants you have is likely to be one or two.

Sharing intimacies is not a cure-all for loneliness and alienation; but the capacity to disclose helps in establishing and sustaining an enduring social relationship. The goal of this book is to explore the factors that foster successful intimate relationships.

We owe a great deal to a number of people who commented on and reviewed various chapter drafts. We gratefully acknowledge the help of Vernon Raschke, Tom Cash, Robert Dies, Kenneth Anchor, and particularly Irv Altman. Barbara Derlega assumed the multiple role of critic, copy editor, and indexer. Zick Rubin, our editor, helped enormously in sharpening "cloudy" chapter drafts. Our wives, Barbara and Dee, provided much-needed morale and ego boosting.

Acknowledgment is due to the individuals we interviewed in preparing the background data for this book. We owe great thanks to Marjorie Bottimore, Peter Powell, Tom Pick, William Lamb, Cliff Saunders, Cletus Cole, and to the students at Old Dominion University who tolerated our questions for the sake of the project. Thank you all.

We would like to give special thanks to Sidney Jourard who conceived of self-disclosure as a legitimate subject of scientific inquiry; his writings inspired us and many other researchers to examine the dynamics involved in the sharing of intimacy. In addition, he was a warm person and a friend. His death in December 1974 was a great shock to all of us. He will be sorely missed.

what is self-disclosure?

After awhile, I felt like I was a part of everyone, and they were a part of me. They really knew me . . . and they still liked me! I found out they all had doubts and fears like me. When it was over, we felt like a family.

—Comments of a participant
following a marathon
encounter group

This book is about self-disclosure, the process by which one person lets himself be known by another person. Decisions about self-disclosure are a constant part of the everyday life of all of us. Should we reveal our thoughts, our feelings, or our past to another person? How intimate should our disclosures be? What are the appropriate places and times to talk about ourselves, and whom should we tell?

The decisions that we make concerning self-disclosure will have great bearing on our lives. Such decisions will determine the number of friends we have and how well we know them. They will influence the extent of our happiness and of the satisfaction we get out of life. To a large extent, our decisions regarding the amount, the type, and the timing of our self-disclosure will affect even the degree of our own self-knowledge and awareness. The anecdotes below explore some of the implications of self-disclosure in different social contexts.

Bill R. has trouble making friends. His acquaintances all like him, but no one knows what he's really like.

Dorothy W. also has no close friends. Unlike Bill, however, she is not reluctant to let others know what she is feeling or what her problems are. In fact, she reveals personal things to almost everyone. People regard her as somewhat strange.

Jim D. feels much closer to Sandy L. after their last date. Sandy finally told him about the problems she had been having with her father, and Jim responded by confessing the jealousy he had always felt toward his older brother. He now knows that his relationship with Sandy has moved to a new, deeper level.

Terry is contemplating a divorce from her husband, Ken. She now realizes that she has never really known him. For five years, she has lived with him, cooked and cleaned for him, and slept with him. In all that time, they have talked only about day-to-day concerns: what was planned for dinner, their weekend plans, and so forth. What is he really like? What are his hopes, dreams, and fears? She really doesn't know.

Arthur M., an executive, is somewhat bewildered as he gets off his plane in Los Angeles. A stranger sat next to him on the flight from New York. After exchanging small talk, the stranger began to tell Arthur about the recent collapse of his marriage. It reminded Arthur of the breakup of his first marriage, and he told the stranger about it. One thing led to another, and before he knew it, Arthur had revealed some feelings and fears that he had never told anyone else before. Arthur doesn't really understand how it happened or why. After all, he will probably never see the man again. Maybe, Arthur thinks, that's why it happened.

John D. has been brooding about the amount of time his wife, Mary, spends at her parents' house. Married for five months, she visits her mother at every opportunity. John feels that his wife and her mother are too close, and that Mary should not tell her mother about their marital problems. But John doesn't tell Mary how he feels: he thinks she should be able to see what the problem is. John has developed moody periods when he picks on Mary. When she asks what is bothering him, John gets angry and clams up.

Michael M. has been seeing Dr. B. in therapy for seven weeks. At first, he had trouble talking about himself, especially his problems at home. Lately, however, it has become easier, and today he is talking about how he resents his parents' attempts to control his life. They've always tried to pick his friends for him, even the girls he dates. It has become much easier for Michael to tell Dr. B. about this ever since the therapist revealed that as a young man, he had had similar problems with his parents. Hearing this made Michael feel closer to Dr. B.; he feels the therapist will understand him and won't think badly of him for having such problems.

As these anecdotes suggest, self-disclosure has implications for anyone interested in how people relate to one another. Clients often ask marriage counselors how they can communicate their feelings more successfully. Two persons may live for years with each other, sharing activities and time but not really knowing each other. An adolescent boy may ask his mother why she doesn't listen to him and why his feelings don't seem to matter to her. Two roommates in a dormitory may ask each other why they are always fighting. How can they settle their differences so that they can get along? Two housewives may spend their mornings talking to each other over the telephone because they feel they can't talk to their husbands. In summary, self-disclosure spans almost every facet of human social behavior. How we relate to other persons, and they to us, is determined by the amount of personal information we and they are willing to communicate.

As the anecdotes imply, self-disclosure can take place on many levels. For example, you can disclose information to another about many areas of your life (large breadth of self-disclosure) and yet reveal only shallow, superficial material (little depth of self-disclosure). You may tell another person that you work in an advertising agency, that you come from Kansas, that you have been married for three years, that you have two older brothers, and that pizza is your favorite food. Such a recital tells the other about many different topics, all related to your life—but the person really knows very little concerning what you feel strongly about, or about your hopes, dreams, and fears, or, in essence, about what makes you unique as a person. Such disclosure is characterized by breadth but not depth. Relationships between casual acquaintances usually follow this pattern. On the other hand, disclosure may be deeply personal and intimate but focus on only one or two areas of one's life, such as sexual feelings or emotions. A summer romance may represent a relationship characterized by depth but not breadth.

In general, intimate disclosure indicates that the discloser trusts his listener. The former has made himself vulnerable by revealing information that could possibly be used to hurt him by an indiscreet listener. In addition, the discloser has left himself open to ridicule or rejection. Such negative consequences could not occur if the discloser reveals only superficial information.

Though less obvious, other cues than just verbal behavior transmit self-disclosure. Nonverbal behavior (duration of eye contact, distance maintained from the listener, gestures, and facial expressions) as well as "paralanguage" (inflections of the voice such as differences in pitch and stress) can convey much information to the observer, especially about such things as the discloser's emotional state, his status, and his liking for the listener. Often, these cues reveal more than does verbal communication.

THE LONELY SOCIETY

Let's consider why self-disclosure assumes so much importance in social relationships. Why do people feel lonely and alienated? Does self-disclosure promote intimacy in social relationships? Can we accelerate friendships by trading secrets?

There is no doubt that loneliness is a central problem for human beings. Joseph Conrad once wrote, "We live, as we dream— alone. . . ." [1] Thomas Wolfe agreed: "The whole conviction of my life now rests upon the belief that loneliness, far from being a rare and curious phenomenon, peculiar to myself and to a few other solitary men, is the central and inevitable fact of human existence." [2]

This existential loneliness is part of living, but it has been greatly aggravated by a number of contemporary developments. Today, loneliness is closely linked to the rise of alienation in modern society. The alienated man is isolated from everything that makes life meaningful—his work, his associates, himself. He feels powerless to influence the course of his own life. He senses that his fate and all the things that happen to him are out of his control. Depressed, confused, and uncertain, the alienated individual withdraws further

---

[1] J. Conrad, "Heart of Darkness," in *Heart of Darkness and The Secret Sharer* (New York: The New American Library, 1950), p. 95.

[2] T. Wolfe, *The Hills Beyond* (Garden City, N.Y.: Sun Dial Press, 1943), p. 186.

and further from the human community. In its extreme forms, alienation may result in suicide or in an individual's being labeled as psychotic and placed in a mental institution. In any form, it leads to loneliness, to feelings of emptiness, isolation, and estrangement.

Why should loneliness and alienation be so widespread? What is there about modern society that fosters these conditions? Actually, the roots of today's alienation were planted several hundred years ago by the onset of two revolutions—one democratic and the other industrial.[3] The democratic revolution created expectations about increased political rights and participation in the system, expectations that were not generally fulfilled. Thus, feelings of powerlessness and resignation proliferated, alienating man from the political process.

The Industrial Revolution initiated a tremendous change in the work habits of masses of people. As a result of the new technology, large quantities of goods could be manufactured cheaply on assembly lines in large factories in central locations. Frequently, workers had to leave their families, as well as the towns in which they had spent their lives, in order to be near their work. Handcrafted products, painstakingly constructed with great pride by skilled artisans, were no longer practical and were priced out of the market. One consequence of this change was the alienation of the worker from his job: he could no longer take pride in his work. The estrangement of people from their jobs and from the political system under which they lived may have been factors in the estrangement of people from one another.

Though the roots of contemporary loneliness are not new, several recent trends in the United States have accelerated the condition dramatically. One new development is the incredible mobility of the modern American. In previous eras, people spent their lives in the towns where they were born, often living in the same house for their entire lives. Everyone in a village knew everyone else; when a person had a problem, his neighbors knew about it almost immediately. People had both physical and psychological roots.

[3] R. Nisbett, *The Social Bond: An Introduction to the Study of Society* (New York: Knopf, 1970).

Such a sense of community is rare in modern America. Americans have become increasingly mobile, even nomadic, in their life styles: the average American moves fourteen times in his lifetime, and about forty million Americans change their home addresses at least once every year.[4] Such a dramatic change in living habits has had a profound effect on friendship patterns, on the family, and on the whole fabric of human interaction.

Although the new mobility represents freedom and psychological growth for many, it has also given rise to loneliness, fear, and isolation. One consequence of the nomadic life style of many Americans has been the severing of family and friendship bonds. The extended family—in which children, parents, grandparents, and even great-grandparents lived in the same household, or at least within short walking distance of one another—has become almost extinct in modern America. Similarly, very few people today retain friendships formed during their childhood.

In addition to increased mobility, urbanization has radically transformed friendship patterns. In large cities, it is common for persons living in adjacent apartments not to know each other's names. Wirth has pointed out that the urbanite forms limited, segmented relationships with others.[5] He knows little about his business associates' personal lives, or his doorman's problems, or the romances of the check-out girl at the supermarket. Such "modularization" makes for efficiency, and indeed is necessary for survival in an urban environment. Unfortunately, it also makes for loneliness.

In an interview in *Psychology Today*, Stanley Milgram, a prominent social psychologist, commented on another alienating phenomenon of urban life, the "familiar stranger."

> For years I've taken a commuter train to work. I noticed that there were people at my station whom I had seen for many years but never spoken to, people I came to think of as familiar strangers. I found a peculiar tension in this situation, when people treat each other as properties of the environment rather than as individuals to deal

[4] V. Packard, *A Nation of Strangers* (New York: McKay, 1972).
[5] L. Wirth, *On Cities and Social Life* (Chicago: The University of Chicago Press, 1964).

with. It happens frequently. Yet there remains a poignancy and discomfort, particularly when there are only two of you at the station: you and someone you have seen daily but never met. A barrier has developed that is not readily broken.[6]

Technology has been a major factor in producing alienation. Alvin Toffler has detailed how the rapid pace of technological and sociological change in our society is a source of physical and emotional stress.[7] People are finding it increasingly hard to cope with social change. Many, feeling powerless and helpless, withdraw from their work and from those who are part of their lives.

Lately, however, there have been stirrings of rebellion against the anonymity and depersonalization of modern life. Increasingly, people are striving to regain feelings of intimacy and community with others. One such sign is the rise of the "group experience" (see Chapter Seven). In a sensitivity-training or encounter group, participants are encouraged to be themselves, to drop the masks and modularizations of normal disclosure, and to find out what they and each of the other group members are really like. Although several writers have warned of the potential dangers in some of these groups, their proliferation attests to the search for intimacy in modern America.

Another example of people trying to achieve intimacy with others was the rise of communal living in the 1960s. By creating an extended family, usually far from the anonymity of the city, and by making do with a minimum of technology, many young people (and some older ones) tried to recover a sense of community with others. A young woman who joined a commune in New Mexico expressed this thought: "When I get up in the morning, I'm happy. I never felt that way before. I know people love me. It's really groovy waking up and knowing that 48 people love you. It gives you all sorts of energy. You're standing alone—but you're standing with 48 people." [8]

[6] C. Tavris, "The Frozen World of the Familiar Stranger: A Conversation with Stanley Milgram," *Psychology Today,* 8 (1974), 70–80.

[7] A. Toffler, *Future Shock* (New York: Random House, 1970).

[8] R. M. Kanter, *Commitment and Community: Communes and Utopias in Sociological Perspective* (Cambridge, Mass.: Harvard University Press, 1972), p. 126.

Some less radical attempts at intimacy occur in many suburbs. Certain persons play the role of "integrator," introducing newcomers to the community by asking them to parties, bridge games, and the like. In other towns, organizations such as churches, women's groups, or civic clubs serve similar functions. Because the resulting friendships may be short-lived, they are made quickly and self-disclosure is superficial. After all, no one is certain who will be the next to move because of a job transfer or a business opportunity in another city. The homogeneity within the typical suburb aids the process of "instant friendship" by acting as a filter to ensure that newcomers resemble other residents in age, socioeconomic class, and even attitudes and values.

In spite of these efforts to accelerate intimacy—encounter groups, communes, integrators and the like—most deep relationships develop gradually. By a process called social penetration, individuals reveal more and more information about themselves, with breadth and depth of disclosure increasing over time. Reciprocal disclosure is another essential in the development of deep interpersonal relationships. As *A* discloses more information about himself to *B*, *B* discloses more information about himself to *A*. Thus, *A* and *B* tend to match each other in their level of disclosure. In both of these processes, a bond of trust develops between the two persons as each steadily reveals more intimate and more guarded material. The role of confidant requires support, warmth, and acceptance of the other's disclosures; the relationship advances only as long as the individuals trust each other.

By emphasizing the importance of self-disclosure in increasing intimacy, we are not writing about the kind of intimacy that requires conformity or excessive dependency. Instead, the closeness derived from sharing one's thoughts should strengthen the individual's resolve to maintain his own identity and self-worth. Baring ourselves to others also makes our periods of privacy much more meaningful and important. We need time by ourselves to reconsider our social relationships, to reflect on the past, and to prepare for future encounters.

WHERE WE GO FROM HERE

In this book, we will explore the role of self-disclosure in everyday life. We will look at the part self-disclosure plays in forming friendships, in the dating relationship, and in marriage. We will also discuss some critical related issues. We will examine how the traditional masculine role of "strong and silent" reduces self-disclosure for most men—and what effects this may have on their physical and mental health. We will examine two new approaches to intimacy—experiential groups and communal living—and the role self-disclosure plays in each.

two

self-disclosure:
is it always healthy?

*Self-disclosure is a symptom of personality health
and a means of ultimately achieving healthy personality.*
—Sidney Jourard

*There's this girl on my floor in the dormitory who's
really weird—she tells people she's just met about really
personal things, like all these guys she's sleeping with.
Everyone tries to avoid her. I think she really needs help.*
—Comments of a coed

Imagine a "low revealer," a person who does not disclose his innermost thoughts, feelings, or problems to anyone, not even to those he loves such as his wife and family. No one, including his family or friends, is at all sure of what he is really like, or who he really is. At parties or at work he is very skilled at small talk, discussing the sports page or his crabgrass. When the conversation turns to more personal concerns, he is able to discuss others' problems or feelings, but he becomes uncomfortable when the conversation turns to him. He may try to deflect the conversation with humor or banter, or he may turn away a question with a question, or he may say nothing at all. Often, his response, or lack of response, may be enough to turn the conversation back to less intimate topics. At home, he tends to maintain an air of mystery about himself. He never says what he is really feeling. His wife discusses her problems with him, but he never reciprocates.

Is this person psychologically healthy? Does a low level of disclosure signify neuroticism? The issue is complex, and the findings are often controversial. The low revealer may take care of his own needs, work hard, pay taxes, and contribute his services to community activities. If mental health is defined as being able to function autonomously, then such an individual is certainly normal. On the other hand, many humanistic psychologists, including Sidney Jourard, Carl Rogers, and Abraham Maslow,[1] distinguish between the "normal" and the "healthy" personality. A person may function effectively in his daily life, and be regarded as normal. Yet as Jourard points out, "Normal personalities are not necessarily healthy personalities." [2]

According to the humanistic psychologists, the healthy person has fulfilled or is close to fulfilling his unique potential as a human being. Maslow calls such a person a "self-actualizer." Self-actualizing human beings experience the world "fully, vividly, selflessly, with full concentration and total absorption." In their choices, they "make the growth choice instead of the fear choice." They understand themselves better than do average people: Maslow states that the self-actualizer "comes to know what his destiny is . . . what his mission in life will be. One cannot choose wisely for a life unless he dares to listen to himself, *his own self,* at each moment in life." For Maslow, the inability to be intimate and honest with at least a few other persons blocks self-growth and prevents the fulfillment of one's potential. As Maslow says in describing steps towards self-actualization, "When in doubt, be honest rather than not." [3]

We believe that one cannot say unequivocally that self-disclosure is either positive *or* negative. The issue is too complex to permit such generalizations. Disclosure can serve a positive function, such as improving a relationship or promoting individual growth, but it may also be inappropriate, such as when it elicits withdrawal or rejection by others. In our view, positive mental health is related to appropriate disclosure, which suits the time, the occasion, and the relationship between the listener and discloser. On the other hand, neurosis and maladjustment appear to be related to inappropriate self-disclosure, such as disclosure that is too intimate (or not intimate enough) for the occasion.

[1] See S. Jourard, *The Transparent Self* (New York: Van Nostrand Reinhold, 1971); C. Rogers, *On Becoming a Person* (Boston: Houghton Mifflin, 1961); and A. Maslow, *The Farther Reaches of Human Nature* (New York: Viking, 1971).

[2] Jourard, *op. cit.,* p. 26.

[3] Maslow, *op. cit.,* pp. 45–46.

It is difficult to define "appropriate" self-disclosure. What is appropriate in one society or in one era may be totally out of place in another. For example, our Victorian ancestors, who referred to "legs" as "limbs" in mixed company, would certainly be horrified at the casual way that many college students discuss sex. In general, disclosure is inappropriate when it conflicts strongly with the prevailing norms concerning the time, place, and context for disclosing various matters. Such a definition is somewhat unsatisfactory; it suggests that nonconformity is inappropriate and, by implication, that it signifies maladjustment. Yet, rigid adherence to social norms can stifle individuality and inhibit psychological growth. Indeed, if norms were never violated, a society would soon stagnate. Still, there seems to be no way to discuss appropriate self-disclosure without reference to social norms—either stated explicitly or understood implicitly—concerning disclosure. In general, persons who completely disregard the norms governing self-disclosure are regarded as maladjusted or deviant by those around them.

In this chapter, we will explore both the positive and negative functions that self-disclosure can serve, and we will examine the reasons why self-disclosure can, depending on the circumstances, be associated with either mental health or maladjustment. We will also discuss some of the guidelines one might use in determining the appropriateness of disclosure.

WHO AM I?

One positive feature of self-disclosure is that it promotes self-awareness. If we hide ourselves from others, then they cannot help us with our problems, nor can they aid us in understanding our unrevealed feelings. Often, a person is afraid that his feelings are unique and that no one else has ever felt the way he does. One encounter group participant, a young woman, told us that until she joined her group she had felt that she was a "monster" because of her angry feelings toward her mother.

> There were times when I just wanted to leave and never see her again. Sometimes I even wanted to hit her. She would keep nagging

me about everything, from finding a husband to cleaning the apartment, until I just felt like screaming. It was really awful. Afterwards, I would feel really guilty about my feelings towards her. After all, she was my mother; she had raised me, and she really did love me. I never told anyone how I felt until I joined the group. Then, when I did, I found that many others in the group had felt the same way at times about their parents. I felt like a big weight had dropped off my back—like I wasn't a horrible person after all.

Knowing that others share similar thoughts and feelings is particularly important in adolescence, when the young person begins to experience new and often frightening feelings. A distinguished psychologist has stated the importance of having a close friend during this period.

In a close relation with a chum these reserved matters can gradually be brought forward and shared, so that not merely one's social front but all of oneself can be compared with another's experience. It can be a great relief to discover that someone else has a similar interior life. One's friend, too, has worried about physical maturation, has felt unattractive, has experienced odd fears and bad dreams, has entertained daydreams of an extravagant sort, and is not in his heart quite the same person that is known to the public. To have another know everything about you is an enlarging experience, provided the confidences are mutual and are given as expressions of love and trust.[4]

Just as others do not know the low revealer, so he does not know others. People are unlikely to reveal themselves wholeheartedly to someone who will not disclose in return. Thus, the low revealer may be unable to perceive the complex motivations and emotions that characterize human beings because his experience with others is limited to superficial contact.

Maslow considers self-knowledge a critical requirement for self-actualization. The low revealer may become cut off, or alienated, from his own being. Not only are others ignorant of his needs and feelings, but, to a great extent, so is he.

When a man does not acknowledge to himself who, what, and how he is, he is out of touch with reality and he will sicken. No one can

[4] R. W. White, *The Enterprise of Living* (New York: Holt, Rinehart and Winston, 1972), p. 298.

help him without access to the facts. And it seems to be another fact that *no man can come to know himself except as an outcome of disclosing himself to another person.* . . . When a person has been able to disclose himself utterly to another person, he learns how to increase his contact with his real self, and he may then be better able to direct his destiny on the basis of this knowledge.[5]

IT HURTS TO KEEP SECRETS

A large discrepancy exists between the low revealer's public self and his true self. To others, the low revealer seems to have no problems or strong emotions. It is difficult for others to see what makes such a person unique, different from everyone else. The low revealer, like all of us, *is* unique. He has problems, feelings, hopes, and fears, even though he may be less aware of them than the average person. When an individual reaches the decision to conceal himself from others, he commits himself to building a false public self. Time, effort, and energy are required to sustain this façade. According to the psychoanalytic viewpoint, each of us possesses only a limited supply of psychic energy. Based on this reasoning, energy that could be used for more constructive activity is channeled into the service of concealment. The person who is totally cut off from his inner feelings may be exhibiting the defense mechanism of repression, an unconscious process. More often, suppression—a conscious act of concealment—is the primary defense. In any case, hiding ourselves from others is an exhausting, full-time job.

The low revealer may be a frightened person, afraid to show himself to others because he lacks trust in their good will. He may be afraid of ridicule, rejection, or the possibility that the listener will reveal the information to others. Rather than risk these negative consequences, an individual may opt for the "safer" course of concealment. In the long run, however, concealment may be more dangerous than disclosure. Jourard argues that the effort involved in maintaining a false public self is extremely stressful, so much so that the nondiscloser may eventually show psychosomatic symp-

[5] Jourard, *op. cit.*, p. 6.

toms, such as ulcers or migraines. One person we interviewed emphasized this point in discussing why she talked about problems to a friend:

> Talking to my friend about my personal problems helps me to get a lot off my chest. My father tends to keep things bottled up, and I also keep things inside. If I can get them out of me, I can feel a lot better. It doesn't nag at my mind.

If we can become open with our feelings, we can cope directly with problems in our social relationships. Otherwise, estrangement and alienation from persons we like and love may result. This failure to communicate may be a problem between dormitory roommates, but it is more serious when it occurs between a married couple. Roommates can always switch partners at the end of the semester, but spouses have no such simple solution to their problems. For example, if a wife is reluctant to disclose to her husband that his habits irritate her, he will continue them, annoying her even more. Eventually, her annoyance may blow out of proportion with devastating consequences.

LEARNING TO BE INTIMATE

Children learn particular patterns of self-disclosure from parents and peers as part of growing up. The child whose parents are warm and open will probably be warm and open himself. The child of secretive, closed parents will likewise use them as models for his own behavior. But at times, a child will rebel by becoming secretive in response to his parents' excessive demands for disclosure. A letter from an upset mother to Ann Landers illustrates this process poignantly:

> Dear Ann Landers: I am a mother who paid a high price for her snoopiness. I was determined that my teenager, Lucille, would never put anything over on me. I read her diary, looked through her bureau drawers, her purse, and her pockets. I eavesdropped on her telephone conversations and did everything imaginable to keep tabs on her. The results were tragic. Lucille became an extraordinary liar. That girl could think up things that would baffle the FBI. Our relationship deteriorated into a bitter contest—Lucille striving to see

how much she could get away with and me figuring out ways to trap her. Finally she wound up in serious trouble. I learned too late that trust and confidence are more effective tools for building honesty than suspicion and investigation. I should have minded my own business.—*Sorry Now*[6]

In societies where children are taught to be suspicious of others, and where such suspicion is justified by the hostile actions of others, self-disclosure is minimal. In a classic early anthropological study,[7] Ruth Benedict described the Dobu tribe of New Guinea. The life style of this tribe was characterized by extreme paranoia. No one trusted anyone else; each tribesman believed that he had to thwart and hurt the other person before the latter did the same to him. In such a society, characterized by the negative golden rule of "Hurt him before he hurts you," it is not surprising that little self-disclosure occurred. In the Dobu tribe, knowledge of a person's hopes and fears would be used against that person by others. If it was known that a particular tribesman was afraid of snakes, he would probably awaken to find a snake in his bed, courtesy of his fellows. Thus, the average Dobu was a secretive person. No one wants his enemies to know him intimately, and to the Dobu tribesman all others were enemies.

Undoubtedly, many low revealers view our own society as the Dobu view theirs. Other persons are seen as potential enemies from whom one's weaknesses must be concealed at all costs. A particularly bitter experience in one's past can also make all kinds of social relationships seem threatening. Erik Erikson, the noted psychoanalyst, has hypothesized that a basic feeling of trust (or mistrust) for others is learned very early in life, and is based on the relationships the young child has with his parents.[8] This early learning may have a profound effect on the child's subsequent patterns of disclosure.

DIARIES, DOGS, AND "RENT-A-BUDDY"

Even when disclosure to another seems impossible, many people may still feel a need to unburden themselves. The great popularity

[6] From the book, *Ann Landers Says: Truth Is Stranger* . . . by Ann Landers. © 1968 by Ann Landers. (Englewood Cliffs, N.J.: Prentice-Hall), pp. 68–69.
[7] Ruth Benedict, *Patterns of Culture* (Boston: Houghton Mifflin, 1934).
[8] E. E. Erikson, *Childhood and Society*, 2nd ed. (New York: Norton, 1963).

of diaries indicates that many people need an outlet for their innermost feelings. Anne Frank wrote that her reason for starting a diary was:

> to bring out all kinds of things that lie buried deep in my heart. . . . The reason for my starting a diary . . . is that I have no . . . real friend.[9]

She adds:

> . . . The brightest spot of all is that at least I can write down my thoughts and feelings, otherwise I would be absolutely stifled! [10]

Like many diarists, Anne Frank would have preferred to confide in another person. Unfortunately, she found herself unable to be open, even with those she loved.

> Let me put it more clearly, since no one will believe that a girl of thirteen feels herself quite alone in the world, nor is it so. I have darling parents and a sister of sixteen. I know about thirty people whom one might call friends—I have strings of boyfriends, anxious to catch a glimpse of me and who, failing that, peep at me through mirrors in class. I have relations, aunts and uncles, who are darlings too, a good home, no—I don't seem to lack anything. But it's the same with all my friends, just fun and joking, nothing more. I can never bring myself to talk of anything outside the common round. We don't seem to be able to get any closer, that is the root of the trouble. Perhaps I lack confidence but anyway, there it is, a stubborn fact, and I don't seem to be able to do anything about it.
>
> Hence, this diary. In order to enhance in my mind's eye the picture of the friend for whom I have waited so long, I don't want to set down a series of bald facts in a diary like most people do, but I want this diary itself to be my friend, and I shall call my friend Kitty.[11]

Obviously, disclosure to a diary cannot accomplish what is probably the most important function of self-disclosure: the creation of an intimate, caring relationship with another person. Yet it does accomplish other important functions. It aids in the clarification of

[9] A. Frank, *The Diary of a Young Girl* (New York: Doubleday, 1953), p. 2.
[10] *Ibid.,* p. 157.
[11] *Ibid.,* pp. 2–3.

one's feelings; one's thoughts and ideas become clearer after they are expressed, either orally or in writing. In addition, there is relief in writing down deeply held feelings that have been bottled up inside, even though no one else may read them.

For similar reasons, some lonely people talk to their pets when there is no one else to confide in. Disclosures to animals may even have certain advantages over disclosures to people; after all, one does not have to worry that his dog will laugh at him or reveal his confidences to others.

Children are especially apt to talk to animals, perhaps because they are less self-conscious. Psychological counselors at the Old Dominion University Child Study Center have capitalized on this fact by constructing a giant "talking dog." This dog, a friendly looking stuffed animal with a two-way radio built into it, is used in work with emotionally disturbed children. A child is left alone with the dog, who "talks" to him via a counselor in the next room. A transmitter inside the dog allows the counselor to hear the child's end of the conversation. Children who are afraid to talk at all to people become extremely open and honest with the "talking dog."

For religious people, God is an ever-present recipient of self-disclosure. Norman Vincent Peale has written "Talk to God simply and naturally, telling him anything that is in your mind. . . . Talk to him in your own language. He understands it." [12]

Future technology may add new wrinkles to the search for persons and things to disclose to. The comedy team of Burns and Schreiber have a routine about a robot called "Rent-a-Buddy." A person can approach it, insert a coin, and then have the machine ask him questions, nod sympathetically, and generally act concerned about him—until the time period ends and another coin has to be inserted.

SIN AND CONFESSION

A different approach to the relationship between self-disclosure and mental health has been proposed by psychologist O. H. Mowrer,[13]

[12] N. V. Peale, *A Guide to Confident Living* (New York: Prentice-Hall, 1948), p. 92.
[13] O. H. Mowrer, "Loss and Recovery of Community: A Guide to the Theory

who views neurosis as a "state of guilt that has neither been admitted nor atoned for." Mowrer agrees with Freud that the core state of neurosis is anxiety and fear, but the two men interpret this anxiety in radically different ways. For Freud, inhibition of behavior, usually because of unrealistic moral constraints, is a prime factor in producing neurosis. The neurotic's ego and superego, the branches of personality concerned with realistic behavior and moral conduct, are in constant conflict with the id, the branch concerned with fulfilling instinctual demands. This conflict provokes anxiety, which the ego deals with by repression, the exclusion from consciousness of the id's demands. Thus, the neurotic is a repressed, inhibited individual.

In contrast, Mowrer sees *suppression,* a conscious decision to withhold the truth about oneself from others, as the "primal pathogenic act." The neurotic, according to Mowrer, is not an inhibited person; indeed, his guilt arises precisely because he did *not* inhibit himself. Instead, the neurotic has "committed an act which is disapproved by the significant others in his life." The neurotic then compounds his guilt by hiding his "sin" from other people. Neurotic behavior or symptoms are then caused by a guilty conscience "when a person of basically good character in some way compromises himself and persistently refuses to do anything about it."

Mowrer advocates self-disclosure in the form of confession of one's "sin" to significant others in one's life as the proper means of therapy for neurosis. He acknowledges that self-disclosure to nonprofessionals, particularly to peers, requires courage. Such disclosure often angers or shocks one's confidants, and punishment frequently results. However, Mowrer sees punishment as a constructive process that may "in its most legitimate form restore the person to full status and fellowship, making him again acceptable and worthy of our cooperation and trust."

Mowrer's approach to neurotic behavior is religious in nature. His concepts of self-disclosure as a means of expiating guilt and of punishment as a restoration process are superficially similar to the

and Practice of Integrity Therapy," in *Innovation to Group Psychotherapy,* ed. G. Gazda (Springfield, Ill.: Charles C Thomas, 1968), pp. 130–89.

Roman Catholic principles of confession and penance. However, Mowrer contends that confession to God, through the agency of a priest, will not relieve neurotic symptoms. Instead, we must seek forgiveness from those persons whom we actually hurt.

Mowrer differs with many theologians on this point. For example, Peale contends that a clergyman is uniquely qualified to receive his parishioner's self-disclosure.

> Remember that the minister is also a professional man. When he is dealing with a human being in the relation of pastor and parishioner, he is applying all of his spiritual, psychological, and scientific knowledge. He is entirely objective, viewing the person whom he is interviewing as a patient to whom he must apply a cure.[14]

Mowrer would reply that it is just this objectivity that prevents the discloser from feeling absolved of his guilt. In supporting his assertion that confession must be to significant others in one's life, Mowrer points out that a fundamental part of the early Christian Church was a procedure called "exomologesis,"

> [which was] a deep, thoroughgoing, unreserved form of self-disclosure, perhaps first to one or two individuals and then to a small group. After this, the individual placed himself "under the judgment" of the group. The group responded to his confession of past wrongdoing with love and compassion, and rejoiced at his new-found honesty and courage. But "forgiveness" was not automatic. The individual, depending upon the nature and extent of his misdeeds, was expected to make restitution, do penance. And when this was accomplished, the person's self-respect returned, his apprehension vanished, and he was restored to the community healed.[15]

With the adoption of Christianity by the Roman Empire in A.D. 325, public confession began to decline; by the twelfth century confession was made privately to an unseen priest. Today, a number of groups within the Catholic church have returned to a confession similar in form to that used by the early church. The confession of parishioner to priest in a confession box is seen by many as inadequate and impersonal; even worse, the penance

14 Peale, op. cit., p. 28.
15 Mowrer, op. cit., p. 135.

imposed does not usually relieve the shame and guilt that the sin has caused.[16]

In our view, Mowrer overstates his case when he asserts that neurosis results from the nondisclosure of wrongdoing. Undoubtedly, guilt over actual transgressions that are concealed from significant others can produce maladjustment. However, there is ample documentation that behavior that might be labeled neurotic —behavior characterized by social anxiety, inadequate interpersonal relationships, impairment in one's work, and so forth—can result from many other causes as well, including guilt over nonexistent (imagined or potential) transgressions.

What is valuable in Mowrer's position is the view that concealment of self occurs out of fear of the consequences of self-disclosure, from a person's belief that if people knew his real self, they would find it ugly and unworthy of love or respect. Mowrer's advocacy of openness and transparency as a path away from fear, guilt, and mental illness represents an important contribution to those who seek positive personality change.

WHEN IT'S GOOD TO CONCEAL

Until now, we have discussed ways in which self-disclosure can promote better interpersonal relationships and mental health. But as we indicated earlier, self-disclosure may also have negative effects and be associated with maladjustment. As early as 1671, a book of etiquette counseled discretion regarding disclosure.

> You will remember that the first rule is never to bring up frivolous matters among great and learned persons, nor difficult subjects among persons who cannot understand them. . . . Do not talk to your company of melancholy things such as sores, infirmities, prisons, trials, war, and death. . . . Do not recount your dreams.

[16] One of the authors (V.J.D.) can remember an experience from his youth that supports Mowrer's position. He had taken twenty-five cents from an older sister's pocketbook. Dutifully, he reported this misdeed at confession to the parish priest, and absorbed the punishment—saying ten Hail Marys. Sadly, confession didn't help. Seeing his sister again, he felt two things: a guilty conscience and fear that she would miss her money.

. . . Do not give your opinion unless it is asked for. . . . Do not attempt to correct the faults of others, especially as that is the duty of fathers, mothers, and lords. . . . Do not speak before thinking what you intend to say.[17]

The value of transparency in social relationships has also been questioned by contemporary critics, such as psychologist Sigmund Koch: ". . . total transparency is constitutive only of nullity . . . [transparent] human beings . . . are among the most boring phenomena in creation." Koch asserts that adherence to the idea of transparency eliminates important qualities of humanity, including ". . . the charm of certain forms of reticence; the grace of certain kinds of containedness . . . the communicative richness of certain forms of understatement, allusiveness, implicativeness, . . . [and] modesty. . . ." [18]

This debate over the value of openness has a long history. Over one hundred years ago, the great German sociologist Georg Simmel wrote of the importance of discretion in human relationships:

Just as material property is, so to speak, an extension of the ego, and any interference with our property is, for this reason, felt to be a violation of the person, there is also an intellectual private property whose violation effects a lesion of the ego in its very center.[19]

Simmel argued that privacy is important: we need to conceal some things in order to maintain the integrity of the person. He also maintained that modern man has become so complex and has been so differentiated into parts and roles that complete intimacy with anyone is virtually impossible to achieve.

Modern man, possibly, has too much to hide to sustain a friendship in the ancient sense. Besides, except for their earliest years, personalities are perhaps too uniquely individualized to allow full reciprocity of understanding and receptivity, which always, after all, requires much creative imagination and much divination which is oriented only toward the other. It would seem that, for all these

---

[17] Cited in P. Ariés, *Centuries of Childhood* (New York: Knopf, 1961).

[18] S. Koch, "An Implicit Image of Man," in L. Solomon and B. Berzon, eds., *New Perspectives on Encounter Groups* (San Francisco: Jossey-Bass, 1972).

[19] K. H. Wolff, ed., *The Sociology of Georg Simmel* (Glencoe, Ill.: Free Press, 1950), p. 322.

reasons, the modern way of feeling tends more heavily toward differentiated friendships, which cover only one side of the personality. . . .[20]

Even when it is possible to be intimate, indiscriminate self-disclosure to everyone one encounters may constitute deviant behavior in our society. An overdiscloser cannot be sure that the listener will respond to his revelations without ridicule or rejection. Indeed, the overdiscloser may find himself rejected. Joseph Luft warns that the "plunger," or too-quick self-discloser, may be regarded as "anathema, to be avoided at all costs." [21] Others may see the plunger as deviant or, at the very least, untrustworthy: if he values his own privacy so little, there is little guarantee that he will value theirs if they should disclose to him. That the plunger repeats his behavior, often in the face of continuing rejection, in itself indicates maladaptive behavior.

An overdiscloser may also find that others have little patience with him. For instance, individuals who always talk about their problems may initially arouse sympathy in their listeners. But listening repeatedly to another's problems becomes unexciting and dull. Sympathy may turn to impatience, and then to annoyance. One coed reported to us her reaction to high revealers; her feelings reflect a prevalent view:

> Sometimes I think that people who tell me personal things about themselves are trying to get sympathy from me, that they are telling me their personal problems so I will say, "Golly, I'm sorry." I don't like that kind of person because I feel they would go and tell their problems to everyone and they wouldn't care if I was a stranger or a friend. To me they can't be very sincere persons.

> There is this one girl at home; she is an orphan, and these people adopted her. She talks all the time about what happened to her and why her real parents didn't keep her and where they are living. She tells about everything that happened to her—like she had an abortion, and she tells people about it. She tells people about her personal things, and they don't want to hear about them. But

---

[20] *Ibid.*, p. 326.

[21] J. Luft, *Of Human Interaction* (Palo Alto, Calif.: National Press Books, 1969), p. 130.

she just wants people to say, "Well, I am sorry," and to feel bad for her.

An important factor in evaluating the healthiness of self-disclosure is the discloser's motive. The high revealer whose disclosures are designed to elicit sympathy is certainly different from (and probably less healthy than) the person whose disclosures are prompted by a desire for genuine intimacy with the other person. Another nonhealthy motive often prompting self-disclosure is "EgoSpeak," a term defined as "the art of boosting our own egos by speaking only about what *we* want to talk about. . . . EgoSpeak is psychological masturbation." [22]

Finally, many writers have stressed the healthiness of solitude. This position is based in part on the belief that we can often discover our true selves better when we are alone. Theologian Paul Tillich wrote that solitude "is the experience of being alone but not lonely . . . to face the eternal, to find others, to see ourselves." [23] And Thoreau noted, "I never found the companion that was so companionable as solitude." [24]

A LOOK AT THE RESEARCH

We have discussed theoretical approaches to self-disclosure and mental health. The reader may be wondering whether any systematic research has been conducted to investigate these speculations. Unfortunately, there is virtually no *experimental* research on this question, although there is a substantial body of correlational studies. A truly experimental study would require a procedure to change the normal level of self-disclosure in different ways for several groups of randomly selected subjects. For example, one group of subjects might be induced to reveal themselves to others at very high levels of intimacy, another group at moderate levels, and a third at low levels. Such a procedure would have to be powerful

[22] E. G. Addeo and P. E. Burger, *EgoSpeak: Why No One Listens to You* (Radnor, Pa.: Chilton, 1973), p. xii.

[23] Cited in Clark Moustakas, *Individuality and Encounter* (Cambridge, Mass.: Howard A. Doyle, 1968), p. 26.

[24] H. D. Thoreau, *Walden* (New York: Random House, 1946).

enough to maintain the particular level of self-disclosure reliably over an extended time period; then, appropriate measures of mental health (including personality tests, clinical interviews, interviews with the subjects' friends and associates, and so on) would be taken on all subjects. In this way, inferences of a *causal* relationship between self-disclosure and mental health (that is, different patterns of self-disclosure cause differences in mental health) could be made. Such a procedure would be difficult to carry out; furthermore, ethical considerations might well preclude such a study. After all, is it ethical for a researcher to implement a procedure which he has reason to believe might generate some emotional disorder in hitherto "normal" subjects? Investigating the relationship in the opposite causal direction—to see if differences in mental health cause differences in self-disclosure patterns—is even more difficult.

Instead of changing a person's customary level of self-disclosure, or his level of mental health, most studies have taken the approach of assessing a subject's usual level of self-disclosure and then observing the correlation[25] between self-disclosure level and some index of mental health. A number of instruments that measure self-disclosure have been constructed. The most widely used has been Jourard's Self-Disclosure Questionnaire (the JSDQ). By assessing persons as low, moderate, or high revealers, the JSDQ and its modifications measure self-disclosure as an enduring personality

---

[25] A correlation refers to a relationship between two events without implying that one is the cause of the other. For example, there is usually a relationship (or correlation) between College Board scores and college grades, high scores being associated with high grades. However, the high scores did not *cause* the high grades, nor did the grades *cause* the scores. Instead, a third factor (or group of factors), such as intelligence, probably caused both high scores and high grades.

In the same way, a correlation between amount of self-disclosure and mental health cannot determine whether self-disclosure *causes* mental health, or if mental health *causes* self-disclosure. However, it can determine if mental health is usually *accompanied* by self-disclosure.

A correlation coefficient is a number ranging from 0 (no relationship) to +1 or −1 (a perfect positive or negative relationship). Correlations under .50 are usually regarded as evidence of a weak relationship between the two events, correlations from .50 to about .70 signify moderate relationships, and correlations over .70 indicate strong relationships.

characteristic. The original questionnaire consists of sixty questions concerning six different areas (for example, attitudes and opinions, the body, and personality). The respondent is asked to indicate on a three-point scale (no disclosure at all, disclosure in general terms, full and complete disclosure) how much he has disclosed about each item in the past, to his mother, his father, his best friend of the same sex, and his best friend of the opposite sex. Three items from the scale, from the topic areas of attitudes, money, and personality, are as follows: (1) my personal views on drinking; (2) how much money I make at my work, or get as an allowance; and (3) the kinds of things that just make me furious.

Although many studies have been conducted to examine the relationship between indexes of mental health—such as scores on such personality tests as the Minnesota Multiphasic Personality Inventory (MMPI) and the Guilford-Zimmerman Temperament Survey—and amount of self-disclosure, the results have been contradictory.[26] Some observers have found positive correlations. One study[27] examined self-disclosure and mental health among trainees for the Peace Corps. An independent assessment team concluded that self-disclosure scores on the JSDQ were positively related to preference by peers for joint assignment and to high ratings on measures of ability to cope with novel situations. In addition, the team found that self-disclosure scores were positively related to cognitive complexity, a personality variable characterized by flexible and open interpersonal functioning. But in spite of these results, the relationship between self-disclosure and these measures was generally weak: none of the correlations was as high as .50.

[26] For example, positive relationships have been reported by P. R. Mayo, "Self-Disclosure and Neurosis," *British Journal of Social and Clinical Psychology*, 7 (1968), 140–48; and D. M. Pederson and K. L. Hisbee, "Personality Correlates of Self-Disclosure," *Journal of Social Psychology*, 68 (1968), 291–98. Negative relationships have been reported by R. W. Persons and P. A. Marks, "Self-Disclosure with Recidivists: Optimum Interviewer-Interviewee Matching," *Journal of Abnormal Psychology*, 76 (1970), 387–91; and P. C. Cozby, "Self-Disclosure, Reciprocity, and Liking," *Sociometry*, 35 (1972), 151–60.

[27] C. F. Halverson and R. E. Shore, "Self-Disclosure and Interpersonal Functioning," *Journal of Consulting and Clinical Psychology*, 33 (1969), 213–17.

Other studies have found negative relationships (that is, low self-disclosure related to positive mental health), and still others have found no relationship at all. How can we account for these different results? First, there is some question regarding the ability of the JSDQ to predict self-disclosure in a real situation. One study found that people whose scores indicated they were high revealers tended to be rated as low revealers by their peers in group counseling sessions.[28] It may be that many people are unable to estimate accurately the amount of their past self-disclosure; or low and high revealers may be reluctant to admit these tendencies on the scale. Second, problems also arise with the concept of "mental health." Does mental health mean the absence of neurotic symptoms? Self-actualization? Productive functioning? Few studies measure this elusive concept the same way.

A third reason for the contradictory results may be that the relationship between self-disclosure and mental health is curvilinear, rather than linear. In other words, very high and very low general levels of disclosure may be associated with poor adjustment, and moderate self-disclosure levels may be correlated with positive mental health. Figure 2-1 shows the nature of this hypothetical relationship. Cozby has noted that if such a curvilinear relation exists, "a positive relationship between disclosure and mental health would be found with samples that contained no high disclosers, while a negative relationship would be found in a sample that contained no low disclosers." Cozby goes on to suggest the following hypothesis: "Persons with positive mental health . . . are characterized by high disclosure to a few significant others in the social environment. Individuals who are poorly adjusted . . . are characterized by either high or low disclosure to virtually everyone." [29]

In support of this hypothesis, a study we conducted found that a person who reveals very personal information to casual acquaintances and strangers was rated as maladjusted by observers. In

[28] J. Hurley and S. Hurley, "Toward Authenticity in Measuring Self-Disclosure," *Journal of Counseling Psychology*, 16 (1969), 271–74.

[29] P. C. Cozby, "Self-Disclosure: A Literature Review," *Psychological Bulletin*, 79 (1973), 73–91.

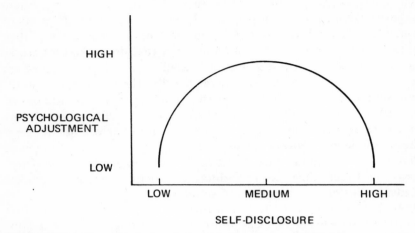

Figure 2–1 Hypothetical relationship between self-disclosure and psychological adjustment.

contrast, persons who reveal themselves intimately to close friends were rated as normal and well adjusted.[30]

GUIDELINES TO DISCLOSURE

The curvilinear hypothesis is related to the point made earlier in this chapter that adjustment is related to appropriate self-disclosure. Whether self-disclosure is appropriate in our society is a function of a number of variables: the context of the disclosure (how it fits in with the ongoing conversation), the recipient of the disclosure (close friend, acquaintance, or stranger; high status or low; young or old), the intimacy of the disclosure, and so on. As Jourard and others have noted, self-disclosure involves great risks. The high revealer is vulnerable to rejection or ridicule, or, at the least, to misunderstanding. His disclosure may be used by the

[30] A. L. Chaikin and V. J. Derlega, "Variables Affecting the Appropriateness of Self-Disclosure," *Journal of Consulting and Clinical Psychology*, 42 (1974), 588–93.

listener to hurt him. Thus, the person who reveals excessively or who reveals to inappropriate persons or at inappropriate times may be showing signs of poor socialization. Such a person has somehow failed to learn the norms governing appropriate self-disclosure. It is easy to see how such an overdiscloser might be less adjusted (or less adaptive) than the person who has learned to disclose at appropriate times and places.

Although most of us, simply by being reared in our culture, have intuitive notions concerning norms of appropriate self-disclosure, little systematic research has been done to examine these norms. One norm, for example, concerns status. Goffman has commented that disclosure by a low-status individual (for example, an elevator operator) to a high-status individual (such as a business executive) is more appropriate than disclosure in the reverse direction.[31] Our own research has confirmed this hypothesis; people view self-disclosure by a person to someone of higher status as more appropriate and less unusual than disclosure to a person of lower status.[32] However, people judge disclosure to a peer as *most* appropriate. The dynamics behind these results may reflect the notion that the discloser is placing himself symbolically on a comparable level with his target. Since few people desire to reduce their status, self-disclosure to a lower-status individual is regarded as somewhat inappropriate and unusual.

Another factor affecting the appropriateness of self-disclosure is the variety of roles that people are forced to play. Goffman suggests that *all* our interactions with others are examples of role playing, and that our performances are designed to create a particular impression on our "audiences."[33] The masks we wear vary, depending on the audience and the type of impression we desire to create. According to this view, we have many "selves" rather than one, and the term "self-disclosure" is thus somewhat misleading.

The appropriateness of different types of self-disclosure depends

[31] E. Goffman, *Interaction Ritual* (New York: Doubleday, Anchor, 1967).

[32] Chaikin and Derlega, *op. cit.* See also D. Slobin, S. Miller, and L. Porter, "Forms of Address and Social Relations in a Business Organization," *Journal of Personality and Social Psychology*, 8 (1968), 289–93.

[33] E. Goffman, *The Presentation of Self in Everyday Life* (New York: Doubleday, 1959).

on the particular role we are playing. As Goffman has noted, it is singularly inappropriate for a salesperson to disclose personal information to a customer unless it is directly related to the transaction. Similarly, intimate self-disclosure by a student to a professor, although much more appropriate than disclosure by professor to student, is inappropriate unless it is relevant to their relationship. For example, it might be appropriate for a student to disclose a personal crisis only if such a recital is necessary to explain why he missed an exam. Sometimes, however, the participants do not agree on the operative norms in the situation. One of our colleagues, an experimental psychologist, told of his amazement when a student in his introductory psychology class talked about his sexual problems during an appointment to discuss an assignment. Apparently, the student perceived the relationship as one of therapist-client rather than student-professor. But other role relationships—such as doctor-patient and priest-confessor—institutionalize and even demand self-disclosure.

Roles often prevent others from finding out about our real selves, including our fears, our weaknesses, and our problems. The more we play a mechanical, artificial role, the harder it is for others to figure out who we really are. Lewis and Streitfeld offer this vivid example of how a role can serve as a protective mask:

> Eddie, a long-haired college student, revealed his primary role as Hip Eddie.
>
> "What do you have to say about yourself, Hip Eddie?" he was asked.
>
> "I'm cool. I smoke pot. I don't give a shit."
>
> "What are you afraid of?"
>
> "That people will get to me."
>
> "How do you mean?"
>
> "That they'll find out about me."
>
> "Find out what?"
>
> "That I'm not what I seem."
>
> "How do you mean?"
>
> "That I've never been laid." [34]

[34] H. R. Lewis and H. S. Streitfeld, *Growth Games* (New York: Bantam, 1972), p. 171.

Luft[35] has provided a number of guidelines for determining the appropriateness of self-disclosure. First, he suggests that self-disclosure is appropriate when it is part of an ongoing relationship. It should not be a random, isolated act. It should develop out of the experiences of the persons involved. It should be reciprocal and mutual. The discloser should monitor and take into account the effect his revelations have on the other person. Above all, the discloser should be wary of revealing information that is too intimate for the present stage of the relationship.

ENCOUNTER IN A CRISIS

Intimate disclosure often occurs between strangers in a crisis. In 1965 a gigantic power failure resulted in a blackout which lasted as long as thirteen hours in some areas in much of the Northeastern United States. Many people were trapped for hours on subways, in elevators, and in transportation terminals. Despite the stress one would expect such an event to cause, many people remember the blackout with pleasure because it generated intimacy with others. For example, one man was quoted in *The New York Times* as saying, "You know, it's a big pain and all, but I sort of hate to see it over. Tomorrow will be just another working day." Pundits and critics marveled over the instant camaraderie and friendship generated by the blackout. *The New York Times* reported that a man asked the conductor on his stalled commuter train to marry him to the girl sitting next to him, whom he had met only a few hours before. The man was reported as believing that the conductor, like the captain on a ship, had the authority to do so.[36]

A blackout or a disaster such as an earthquake often strips away the customary norms governing social discourse. Intimate self-disclosure becomes possible, and sometimes even necessary, as a way of bolstering one's confidence and reducing one's fear. Stanley Schacter has shown that fear tends to increase one's desire to be with others; part of this desire is a wish to study others in the same

---

[35] Luft, *op. cit.*
[36] *The New York Times,* November 10, 1965.

situation.[37] This permits a person to gauge just how much fear is appropriate in the situation at hand. Thus, self-disclosure among persons caught in a crisis often begins with disclosures about how one feels at the moment. In this way, a group can share one another's emotions, especially fear and anxiety, making it easier for each individual to cope with his own feelings. Self-disclosure may then progress naturally to other topics. This is especially likely if people are trapped together for long periods of time with nothing else to do but talk, as in the case of the 1965 Blackout.[38]

THE RECIPROCITY NORM AND MENTAL HEALTH

Self-disclosure is also appropriate when it is made in response to another's self-disclosure. As we shall discuss at length in Chapter Three, "self-disclosure begets self-disclosure." The one variable that allows us to predict the intimacy of X's disclosure to Y with the greatest accuracy is the intimacy of Y's prior disclosure to X. With this in mind, we decided to run an experimental study[39] to test the hypothesis that neurotic individuals are less likely to adhere to this "reciprocity norm" than well-adjusted persons. Our hypothesis was based on the notion that mental health is related to appropriate self-disclosure. The maladjusted individual should be less likely to conform to societal norms about when intimate self-disclosure is called for and when it is not. Some support for our hypothesis exists in a study conducted in Britain which found that two thirds of sample patients hospitalized for neurosis or "nervous breakdowns" reported that they disclosed more to others than others did to them. In contrast, only one third of a control group of normal persons reported such nonsymmetrical disclosure.[40]

To explore these ideas, we administered the Maudsley Personal-

[37] S. Schacter, *The Psychology of Affiliation* (Stanford, Calif.: Stanford University Press, 1959).

[38] Actually, there *were* other things to do. An increase in the birth rate in New York City was recorded exactly nine months after the Blackout took place.

[39] A. L. Chaikin, V. J. Derlega, B. Bayma, and J. Shaw, "Neuroticism and Disclosure Reciprocity," *Journal of Consulting and Clinical Psychology*, in press.

[40] P. R. Mayo, "Self-Disclosure and Neurosis," *British Journal of Social and Clinical Psychology*, 7 (1968), 140–48.

ity Inventory (MPI)[41] to about one thousand undergraduates. The MPI is a widely used scale that examines two major dimensions of personality: extroversion-introversion and neuroticism. The latter is defined by Eysenck, the scale's originator, as the "general emotional instability of a person, his emotional overresponsiveness, and his liability to neurotic breakdown under stress." Research has indicated that the scale has considerable accuracy in identifying persons who have been diagnosed as neurotic by psychiatrists or psychologists, or by other personality tests. Some of the items on the scale that assess neuroticism are listed below. Respondents are asked to check "Yes," "No," or "Uncertain" for each item.

Do you sometimes feel happy, sometimes depressed, without any apparent reason?

Are you inclined to ponder over your past?

Have you often lost sleep over your worries?

Do ideas run through your head so that you cannot sleep?

We asked about fifty males of the original one thousand that were given the MPI to come to our laboratory for an experiment. Of those called, half were "normal," based on their MPI scores, and the remainder were "neurotic," ranking very much higher than average on the neuroticism scale.

Each subject came by himself to the lab, where he was greeted by the experimenter and asked to sit in a "phone booth." All instructions were administered by telephone. The experimenter explained that this was an experiment to discover how persons form impressions of others and that he, the subject, would be asked to describe himself to another subject already in the lab. The other subject would also describe himself. The two would never meet, it was explained, so as to facilitate candor.

In reality, the other subject was a confederate who was "programmed" to tell either very intimate things about himself (sexual feelings, feelings about his father, times he had cried as an adult, and so on) or very superficial things (such as the church he attended, or why he liked his apartment). "By chance," the confederate always spoke first. Following this, it was the subject's turn to talk about himself.

[41] H. J. Eysenck, *The Maudsley Personality Inventory* (San Diego: Educational and Industrial Testing Service, 1962).

What would our subject disclose about himself? He had just heard a stranger reveal information that was either very personal or very superficial. He knew he would never meet the stranger. Would his own disclosure be intimate? This was the main focus of the study.

Each subject's self-disclosure was tape-recorded [42] and later analyzed for level of intimacy by two independent judges who were ignorant of the hypothesis and design of the experiment. Our results are shown in Figure 2–2. Subjects with normal scores on the MPI followed the reciprocity norm. When the confederate disclosed intimate information to them, they were likely to reciprocate with information that was also intimate. When the confederate was superficial, so were they. Neurotic subjects did not seem to take the confederate's level of intimacy into account in formulating their own self-disclosure. Figure 2–2 shows that the intimacy level for neurotics was moderate and was approximately the same regardless of the intimacy of the confederate's initial self-disclosure.

Neurotics either may be unaware of norms prescribing when people should disclose and when they should not, or they may be aware of them and still fail to observe them. They do not seem to take situational cues into account: in some situations calling for low disclosure, neurotics may overdisclose. In situations when high self-disclosure is appropriate, they may underdisclose. In either case, their behavior may prevent them from forming meaningful relationships with others. If they overdisclose at the wrong time in the wrong place to the wrong person, they will elicit rejection and withdrawal. On the other hand, many neurotics may be unable to form close attachments with other persons because they fail to disclose themselves when it is appropriate to do so as part of a developing relationship.

Why have neurotics developed such maladaptive patterns of self-disclosure? Perhaps the neurotic is so preoccupied with his own defenses, anxiety, and problems that he simply does not perceive situational cues that should influence his behavior. Or the neurotic individual may have a history of such unsatisfactory interpersonal

---

[42] For a discussion of ethical issues involved in this procedure, see Chapter Eight.

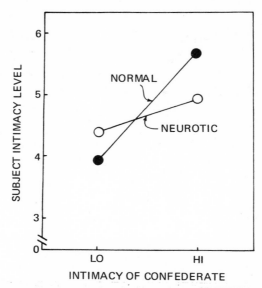

Figure 2–2 Intimacy of self-disclosure as a function of intimacy input and neuroticism. (From A. L. Chaikin, V. J. Derlega, Ben Bayma, and Jacqueline Shaw, "Neuroticism and Disclosure Reciprocity," *Journal of Consulting and Clinical Psychology.* Reprinted by permission of the American Psychological Association.)

relationships that he has developed a pattern of moderate self-disclosure, regardless of the situation. With such a pattern, he may reason, he will not be labeled cold and superficial, as he might if he didn't disclose at all; at the same time, he will not risk the ridicule and rejection that may result from overdisclosure, especially disclosure of deviant information. In any case, one aspect of psychotherapy for the neurotic might involve training in discriminating situational cues related to appropriate levels of self-disclosure.

Is Self-Disclosure Healthy?

There is no simple answer to this question. There are occasions when self-disclosure improves a relationship between two persons and makes them closer, or when disclosure becomes a path to self-awareness and self-actualization. At other times, such as very early in a relationship, too intimate disclosure will make the other person withdraw or even terminate the relationship. In our view, one characteristic of the adjusted, healthy person is the ability to discriminate between situations where disclosure is appropriate and situations where it is not.

three

disclosure reciprocity: you tell me your dreams and I'll tell you mine

You're a commuter about thirty-five years old. One evening, you're settling down in your seat on the train with your newspaper for the ride home. A man walks up to your seat, says "Hi," and sits down next to you. You recognize him as Jim Bryant, a neighbor who lives down your block, but you really don't know him more than to say hello to on the street. Vaguely, you remember that your young son plays ball with his son.

After exchanging some opening remarks ("I didn't know you took this train, Jim." "Yes, well, usually I don't, but I got through a little early at the office today.") and some small talk ("Hey, I saw your boy at the Little League last week. He's getting to be quite a hitter!" "Well, thanks! Your kid's no slouch either!"), you notice that Bryant seems rather nervous, even upset. You wonder what's the matter, but, respecting his privacy, you say nothing.

Then, after a period of silence, Bryant turns to you and says, "You know, kids are funny. You raise them, you do everything for them, and then they go out and do something that breaks your heart." Startled, you ask him what he means. "Well, you know Amy, our oldest? She's seventeen and going to graduate from high school this year. Well, we've told everyone that she decided to complete her senior year at her cousin's school, out in California. But that's not what happened at all." He pauses.

"It's not?" you ask.

"No. She decided to run off with this guy she's been seeing. We didn't even know where she was for three months. The police were looking for her, as a missing person—she might have been dead for all we knew. They finally traced her to this commune in New Mexico. They're living off the land—that and checks some of the parents send the kids. She's written us for money and my wife thinks we ought to send her some, but I can't see it—it would just encourage her to stay there. Maybe with no money they'd make her leave and she'd have to come home. You know, I never would have thought Amy could do something like this. It's just unbelievable . . . I don't know why I'm telling you this. We haven't told any of our friends the truth."

How would you feel if you were Jim Bryant's confidant? You probably would feel a mixture of things—embarrassment, perhaps, or sympathy. You might feel warmer toward Jim for trusting you enough to confide in you. One thing you might do is reciprocate, by telling him something about yourself or your family. Before long, you might find yourself confiding personal problems, aspirations, or fears to Bryant, something you never would have done if he hadn't confided in you first. By the time you both left the train you would probably feel much closer to each other.

One consistent finding in the research on self-disclosure is that disclosure by one person elicits self-disclosure from another person: a person's intimate disclosure encourages intimate disclosure by his listener, and superficial disclosure encourages superficial disclosure in return. Many studies[1] have found evidence for disclosure reciprocity, what Sidney Jourard calls the "dyadic effect." Some theorists view reciprocity as the critical process by which friendships are formed and strengthened. According to this view, friendship begins when one person risks possible ridicule or rejection by

---

[1] See, for example, S. Jourard and R. Friedman, "Experimenter-Subject 'Distance' and Self-Disclosure," *Journal of Personality and Social Psychology,* 25 (1970), 278–82; M. Worthy, A. Gary, and G. Kahn, "Self-Disclosure as an Exchange Process," *Journal of Personality and Social Psychology,* 13 (1969), 59–64; and P. C. Cozby, "Self-Disclosure, Reciprocity, and Liking," *Sociometry,* 35 (1972), 151–60.

disclosing some personal information about himself to the other. The second person reciprocates by sharing something equally intimate about himself. The first person then responds, either at that time or at a later meeting, by revealing something more intimate about himself. In turn, this elicits a comparable disclosure from the other person. Little by little, in a spiraling fashion, this reciprocal exchange builds and strengthens bonds of intimacy, understanding, and trust between the two persons. There are two factors that can abort this developing relationship. First, neither party may be willing to initiate an intimate exchange. Second, the recipient of an intimate disclosure may clam up and not reciprocate.

Why does disclosure reciprocity occur? If I tell you something personal about myself, why should that lead you to respond with an intimate disclosure of your own? One popular explanation, which might be labeled the "social attraction" position, postulates that being entrusted with another's disclosure is considered to be a social reward by the listener. Since intimate disclosures are usually shared only by close friends, the initial disclosure may be viewed by the recipient as a sign that he is liked and trusted: "Imagine—he told me such personal things about himself. With all these people in the office that he could have talked to, he felt that he could trust me the most." A scene from a recent novel illustrates this same process. A policeman has told his partner about a robbery he committed, and the partner reacts in this way:

> But I could understand why Joe hadn't been able to stop himself from telling at least one other person about it, and I was kind of flattered I'd been the one he picked. I mean, we'd been friends for years, we lived next door to each other, we worked out of the same precinct, but when a guy trusts you with a secret that could put him away for twenty years you *know* you've got a friend.[2]

As many studies have shown, one factor leading person A to like person B is A's belief that B likes him. According to this theory, the listener likes the discloser for confiding in him and displays his liking by disclosing intimate material in return. The following

[2] D. Westlake, *Cops and Robbers* (New York: M. Evans, 1972), p. 19.

sequence of events summarizes the social attraction explanation of disclosure reciprocity:

1. A reveals intimate information to B.
2. B infers that A's disclosure was based on his liking for him.
3. B likes A.
4. B reveals intimate information to A.

The social attraction position makes sense intuitively, but studies have suggested that steps 2 and 3 may not be necessary for disclosure reciprocity to occur. B may reciprocate A's disclosure even in the absence of liking. The skeptical reader may be thinking, "But do you mean that I am going to match intimacies even if I don't like the person?" We conducted a study[3] to answer this question. The study was designed to determine if intimate self-disclosure by A would lead to similar disclosure by B, even if the content of A's disclosure was designed to make B dislike her. We arranged a setting in which two college women met for the first time in what was described as an experiment on "impression formation." Each subject was told that she would be asked to talk about herself to the other. Actually, one woman was a confederate who always delivered the same disclosure. The other woman was the actual subject. Although the subject believed that the choice of first speaker was due to chance, the study was arranged so that the confederate spoke first every time.

One third of the subjects heard the confederate talk about herself in a superficial, nonintimate manner. She discussed plans for a summer vacation and a family reunion. Another third of the subjects heard her provide the following highly intimate information:

> Well, I don't know exactly what you want me to talk about, but I'll just start with what's been on my mind a lot all week, okay? I've really been troubled about my relationship with my best friend. Something really embarrassing happened to us last week that just seems to have changed our feelings for each other. I don't know what's wrong with me, maybe I'll be all right in a few weeks, but I

[3] V. J. Derlega, M. Harris, and A. L. Chaikin, "Self-Disclosure Reciprocity, Liking, and the Deviant." *Journal of Experimental Social Psychology*, 9 (1973), 277–84.

feel very alienated from him right now. Well, I guess since I've started talking about it, I should tell you what it is that happened, even though it's kind of personal.

Bill and I have been real close for almost two years now. We both came to State U. from high school so we could be together. Lately, we've been getting very involved sexually, but it's hard to find the time and place to be together because we're both living with our parents. Well, I don't really feel too guilty about this, because Bill and I are very serious about each other, and he's the only one I've ever had sex with, but my mom and dad are very religious, and . . . anyway, my mother walked in on Bill and me last week while we were on the living room sofa with our clothes off, and, well . . . you can guess the rest. It was such a bad scene! I really got upset! She called me names that I never expected to hear from my own mother. I know it was a dumb thing for us to do, but my parents were asleep and, well, I don't know . . . it was just awful! I haven't been able to think of anything else since it happened, and Bill and I are arguing. I just feel so alienated from him because she made me feel so cheap and guilty. I don't even want to see Bill for a while, and he can't understand how I feel. Wow! I'm sorry I got so carried away, I'm sure my time is up. I think I've said enough!

The remaining third of the subjects heard the confederate (always played by the same actress) reveal the same intimate information— but this time her lover was named Betty, and her relationship was a homosexual one.

We felt confident that our subjects would like our confederate more when she revealed details of a heterosexual relationship than when she disclosed a homosexual relationship. As we expected, confessing to a Lesbian relationship did not endear our confederate to the subjects. A long line of research in social psychology has demonstrated that people dislike and reject others who are dissimilar to themselves, especially persons who deviate from societal norms of proper behavior. In our study, the homosexual confederate was liked less than either the heterosexual confederate or the confederate who revealed superficial information. The critical question was whether the subjects would reciprocate and reveal intimate material to a person who was not liked. To our surprise, subjects who had listened to the Lesbian confederate were willing to divulge slightly *more* intimate information than subjects who had listened to the heterosexual confederate, and considerably more than subjects who had listened to the superficial confederate.

These results show that liking cannot always account for disclosure reciprocity, for the effect occurred even when the first discloser was not liked. Another study[4] has found similar results, giving us additional confidence in our conclusion.

Since reciprocity occurs even in the absence of liking for the initial discloser, how else, then, can we account for it? One distinguished sociologist proposed that a norm of reciprocity governs much of our social behavior.[5] Operating in a *quid pro quo* manner, people often feel obligated to return the services they have received from others—whether money, favors, or disclosures. Rejected suitors may exploit this principle to their own advantage: "Listen, I spent all this money on you, you can't just say 'good night' now!" If a person does not or cannot reciprocate in an equivalent manner, he will feel unhappy, anxious, and may even dislike his "benefactor." It has been suggested, for example, that the inability of other nations to repay the United States for its foreign aid may be a causal factor in anti-American sentiment in those countries.

Underlying the notion of a reciprocity norm is the assumption that people wish to preserve equity, or equality, in their social relationships.[6] If a person feels that he is always on the giving end of a relationship, he will become resentful and angry. Examples of this include the employee who feels he is underpaid by his boss or the host who always has a friend over for dinner but is never invited in return; the employee may quit, or work less, and the host may terminate the relationship, or at least stop issuing dinner invitations to his friend. In other words, there will be a tendency to reestablish equity.

Although it may not be as strong, the individual on the receiving end of an inequitable relationship will also feel uncomfortable. Few

---

[4] Cozby, *op. cit.*

[5] A. W. Gouldner, "The Norm of Reciprocity: A Preliminary Statement," *American Sociological Review*, 25 (1960), 161–78.

[6] For a discussion of equity theory, see J. S. Adams, "Inequity in Social Exchange," in L. Berkowitz, ed., *Advances in Experimental Social Psychology*, Vol. 2 (New York: Academic, 1965).

people like to feel that they are in debt to another or that they are exploiting someone. Thus, a move toward equity may originate with the party who is reaping the rewards from the inequity. By failing to reciprocate, the recipient of high disclosure places himself and the discloser in an inequitable situation. The discloser has invested more in the relationship in the form of high self-disclosure than has the listener.

An additional reason for seeking equity concerns the difference in power between the discloser and the listener who fails to reciprocate. The latter has learned some potentially damaging information. He can use it to malign the other's reputation or to blackmail him if he is so inclined. The initial discloser lacks the power to retaliate. Since inequity is unpleasant to both parties, reciprocity is likely to occur.

One study we conducted suggests that people may dislike those who violate the reciprocity norm.[7] Subjects watched a video tape of two persons conversing. One girl revealed something about herself, then the other girl replied. When the second girl's disclosure was equal in intimacy to the first girl's, she was liked. This result occurred as long as the second girl's disclosure matched the first girl's, regardless of whether the first girl had been very superficial or somewhat intimate; however, when the second girl's intimacy level differed from the first's, either by being much more or much less intimate, she was disliked. If the second girl was more intimate than the first, our subjects thought she was maladjusted and unusual. When she was less intimate than the initial discloser, she was perceived as cold and unfriendly. These results suggest that people may conform to the reciprocity norm in order to be liked.

MODELING: THE POWER OF IMITATION

Zick Rubin of Harvard University has proposed a two-part theory of reciprocity, based on the principles of modeling and trust. Rubin writes that modeling may mediate reciprocity: "Especially when norms of appropriate behavior are not clearly defined, people look

[7] A. L. Chaikin and V. J. Derlega, "Liking for the Norm-Breaker in Self-Disclosure," *Journal of Personality*, 42 (1974), 117–29.

to one another for cues as to what sort of response is called for." [8] In other words, people use the behavior of others as a guide to how they should behave. If one person discloses something intimate, the other person is likely to use the disclosure as a model and respond in kind.

Modeling is especially apt to occur in laboratory experiments. Here, a subject is in an unfamiliar setting. He is unsure of what to do or what is expected of him, except for some vague words from the experimenter about studying "impression formation" or "person perception." When the "other subject" (who is typically an actor or actress working for the experimenter) speaks first, the subject uses the confederate's conversation as a guide for his own responses.

This possibility suggests that some demonstrations of disclosure reciprocity might just be laboratory "artifacts," by-products of the procedures used in psychology experiments. One social psychologist has theorized that subjects in a psychological experiment want to be "good subjects"; their main concern is behaving in the way the experimenter expects them to behave.[9] Since the experimenter may deliberately disguise the actual purpose of his study (in order to ensure that the subjects' behaviors are "natural"), the subject assumes the role of detective. He searches the experimental situation for clues ("demand characteristics") that will tell him how to behave. One prominent clue in a disclosure reciprocity study is the level of disclosure of the first subject (or confederate). The modeling process may thus be a response to demand characteristics: "Aha, this guy is being very intimate (or superficial) in his self-description. I guess that's the way the experimenter wants me to act, too!"

Nevertheless, there is evidence that disclosure reciprocity in the laboratory is not simply an attempt to please the experimenter. A study we conducted suggests that disclosure reciprocity occurs even in the absence of demand characteristics from the experimental

---

[8] Z. Rubin, "Lovers and Other Strangers: The Development of Relationships in Encounters and Relationships," *American Scientist,* 62 (1974), 182–90.

[9] M. T. Orne, "On the Social Psychology of the Psychological Experiment: With Particular Reference to Demand Characteristics and Their Implications," *American Psychologist,* 17 (1962), 776–83.

situation.[10] In our study, half of the subjects (female college students) believed that they were participating with another woman (actually an actress who was a confederate of the experimenters) in an experiment on person perception in which they would exchange self-descriptions. The confederate always talked first, in either an intimate or a nonintimate manner. In this experimental condition, demand characteristics were high.

The other half of the subjects were led to believe that they were going to watch videotapes as their role in the study. Before the tapes were shown, the experimenter suddenly "remembered" that he had to get some forms from another building. He left the room, whereupon the actress (always the same college-age woman), began to talk "spontaneously" about herself, delivering either the same low- or high-intimacy disclosures used in the high-demand conditions. In this situation, no demand characteristics should have existed, since the subjects thought that the confederate's disclosure was unrelated to the study. In all conditions, the subjects' return disclosures (if any) were recorded surreptitiously and then rated for intimacy by two judges who were "blind" to (that is, ignorant of) the subjects' experimental conditions.

Here are some examples of subject disclosures following the low-intimacy disclosure by the actress. She mentioned that she was studying for an exam that day in a Russian course and that the course was quite difficult:

> Yeah, I know what you mean. Some of the courses here are really difficult, especially the language—I had German last term and I couldn't wait to get it over with.

> I'm just waiting to get out of here so I can go to the beach. It looks like a good day for getting a tan. I'm really pale too. I hope this won't take too long.

> Last week was my bad time for exams. This week I'm just taking it easy and relaxing.

In contrast, here are some representative disclosures following the actress's high-intimacy disclosure, in which she described problems with her parents over a sexual relationship she was having with her boyfriend:

---

[10] V. J. Derlega, A. L. Chaikin, and J. Herndon, "Demand Characteristics and Disclosure Reciprocity," *Journal of Social Psychology*, in press.

You think you have problems! Last week my parents put my kid sister in a mental hospital. For the last month she just stayed in her room and cried. We don't even know why. She won't eat, won't go to school . . . so the doctor said we should put her in this hospital. They may try shock therapy. We're all sick about it.

Parents can be a real pain. Mine gave me hassles about the guys I saw too. Finally, I just moved out. There comes a point when you just have to say to yourself, "That's all the shit I'm going to take!"

I don't believe in premarital sex at all. I know you may think that's strange, these days, but God put us here to live as morally as we can and that's what I'm trying to do.

As these examples illustrate, reciprocity occurred in both low- and high-demand conditions. In other words, subjects were more intimate in their own disclosures when they responded to an intimate disclosure by the confederate than when they responded to a superficial disclosure, even when no demand characteristics were present.

A "demand" unrelated to experimental demand characteristics may underlie the disclosure reciprocity norm. That is, intimate disclosure by another may be perceived by the listener as an implicit demand by the discloser that she reciprocate in kind. For example, imagine two persons on a blind date. If the male tells his date some intimate information about himself, such as the fact that his parents are getting a divorce, his date may feel pressured to reveal something equally intimate in return. If she does not, she may feel that her date will decide that she doesn't like him. She may then accede to his "demand" for an intimate disclosure even though she doesn't really want to disclose herself fully at this early stage of their relationship.

WHOM DO YOU TRUST?

Modeling of intimate self-disclosure is unlikely to occur if one does not trust the first discloser. Irwin Altman of the University of Utah notes that if trust exists, the discloser "expects his disclosure to be received in an accepting, nonthreatening way and/or that some positive consequence will follow, e.g., social approval, heightened compatibility, etc." [11] Another person's disclosure to us is a powerful cue indicating that we can trust him:

> When another person reveals himself to you, you are likely to conclude that he trusts you. He has, after all, made himself vulnerable to you, entrusting you with information about his feelings and experiences which he would not ordinarily reveal to others. A common response in such a situation is to demonstrate to the other person that his . . . trust [is] well-placed. One effective way to do this is to disclose yourself to him in return, implicitly telling him, "I will not be your therapist or confessor—I will allow you to know as much about me as you have allowed me to know about you." [12]

At this point, you may be wondering if disclosure reciprocity occurs every time an initial discloser reveals information about himself. Surely, there must be situations, you may be thinking, in which reciprocal disclosure is inappropriate and unlikely, or where an intimate revelation elicits withdrawal rather than reciprocal intimacy. For example, certain role relationships, such as priest-confessor or doctor-patient, discourage mutual disclosure. Meetings between peers may also fail to show reciprocity for various reasons. For instance, if a person believes that his disclosure will lead to rejection or ridicule by the listener, or that it will be made public, or that it will be used later to hurt him, he may not reveal intimate information, regardless of the level of intimacy of the other person's prior disclosure.

An excellent literary example of the potential negative consequences of self-disclosure reciprocity is found in the play, *Who's Afraid of Virginia Woolf?* [13] George and Martha have invited Nick and Honey to their house for after-party drinks. With their wives elsewhere temporarily, George reveals to Nick some intimate information about his adolescence. Nick reciprocates by revealing to George that Honey's hysterical pregnancy forced him to marry her. A few hours later, George, who feels that Nick has humiliated

---

[11] I. Altman, "Reciprocity of Interpersonal Exchange," *Journal of the Theory of Social Behavior*, 3 (1973), 249–61.

[12] Rubin, *op. cit.*

[13] E. Albee, *Who's Afraid of Virginia Woolf?* (New York: Atheneum, 1966).

him, plans his revenge. He declares that the two couples will play
the game of "Get the Guest"; this involves George's telling everyone what Nick told him earlier about Honey's hysterical pregnancy. Honey is stunned and becomes ill. She rushes off to the
bathroom and everyone, except George, is irritated and embarrassed. The scene ends with Nick vowing to make George regret
his behavior.

This account describes in an extreme way how personal information can be used against the discloser. It suggests that the mutual
disclosure of intimate information may not occur if the individuals
do not trust each other completely, or if one feels that his disclosure
could result in negative consequences for him. Dalmas Taylor,
Irwin Altman, and Richard Sorrentino investigated the effects of
lack of trust between two persons on their self-disclosure.[14] A
confederate interacted with a subject over an intercom for four
forty-five-minute sessions. He varied the kind of feedback he
provided, according to different conditions: feedback was either
favorable and approving or unfavorable and disapproving. For
example, to the subject's statement that "I become panicky in tight
situations," favorable (positive) feedback was: "I know what you
mean. If you are in an accident or even get caught doing something
wrong, things can get pretty panicky." Unfavorable (negative)
feedback consisted of this response: "I don't know what you mean.
If I'm in a tight situation, I try to think things out calmly.
Becoming panicky is a bad thing."

Positive feedback indicated to the subjects that they could trust
the confederate with intimate information; on the other hand,
negative feedback was a sign that the confederate could not be
relied on to receive the subject's disclosure "in an accepting,
nonthreatening way." As the authors predicted, disclosure, in terms
of length of time talking as well as variety and level of intimacy of
the topics that subjects were willing to reveal, was generally higher
in the favorable than in the unfavorable feedback conditions.

[14] D. Taylor, I. Altman, and R. Sorrentino, "Interpersonal Exchange as a
Function of Rewards and Costs and Situational Factors: Expectancy Confirma-
tion-Disconfirmation," *Journal of Experimental Social Psychology,* 5 (1969), 324–39.

Drawing by Charles Schulz; © 1962 United Feature Syndicate, Inc.

IT'S DIFFERENT IF YOU'RE FRIENDS

Virtually all the research reported in this chapter deals with relationships between strangers. Can we really apply any of the previously mentioned findings to long-term relationships? After all, brief encounters between strangers do not involve the risks—or the benefits—that characterize extended relationships between friends, relatives, and co-workers.

Rubin argues that it *is* possible to extrapolate the findings of studies concerned with disclosure reciprocity between strangers to processes involved in the formation of friendships and other intimate relationships.[15] He cautions, though, that in drawing such analogies we must bear in mind some essential differences between the two situations. For example, a relationship between two friends extends across time and space: it exists even when the two are apart. In contrast, an encounter between strangers exists only during a short time and in a single location. The transient nature of such an encounter may affect the content and style of their disclosures.

Nevertheless, Rubin contends (and we agree) that the study of encounters between strangers can provide insights into the way intimate, long-term relationships are developed and maintained. After all, every relationship is composed of a series of encounters; a meeting between two strangers may have similarities to the continuing meetings of friends or lovers. For example, in interactions between both strangers and friends, monitoring of each other's behavior takes place. The discloser is always alert to the listener's reactions (approval? ridicule? rejection?) whether the two have just met or are already good friends.

There are reasons why patterns of self-disclosure reciprocity might be different for strangers than for friends. First, the obligation to reciprocate disclosure may be stronger between strangers than between friends. In the early stages of friendship, reciprocity is necessary to prove one's trust and to advance the relationship to a new stage. But in the later stages, when two persons are close

---

[15] Rubin, *op. cit.*

friends, trust has already been established: a person can respond to his close friend's intimate disclosure by probing deeper and by dealing with the issue that has been raised, knowing that his friend's trust and affection will not be adversely affected by his failure to reciprocate immediately. *Second, a person's knowledge of his friend's personality, interests, and attitudes will enable him to decide realistically what information should be shared. For example, one girl told us of her misgivings in divulging certain information about herself to a close friend:

> We're really close—we tell each other almost everything. The only thing I hold back on is telling her about sex. She's had some bad experiences, and she's really uptight and prudish about it, so I just don't tell her much about that part of my life.

Even in advanced stages of relationships, it is probably true that mutual self-disclosure is still the rule, though with a longer time perspective. That is, although a friend is not obliged to reciprocate self-disclosure immediately, the relationship will usually deteriorate if an overall level of mutuality is not maintained over the long run.

In the formation of new friendships, the reciprocal nature of self-disclosure becomes critical. In Chapter Four, we will find that the mutual sharing of personal information is a key ingredient in the development of long-term relationships.

four

getting close:
how we make friends

*Durable, dependable friendships grow out of
association, a degree of intimacy which allows us to see
and know each other as we really are; and in revealing
our true selves to each other, we find the real test of
friendship.*
—Dave E. Smalley

Think of all the people you see and meet every day—your
neighbors, your school friends, fellow commuters, fellow office
workers, and your family. We know by sight perhaps several
hundred persons, and we say hello to many of them. However, the
number of persons we are likely to know intimately is small, and
some of us cannot even claim a few confidants.

The enormous changes in American society have increased the
number of persons whom we meet, but these relationships tend to
be superficial and casual. The increasing mobility of our society
reduces the likelihood of intimacy in social contacts. Many
relationships remain deliberately superficial in order that their
short-term durability may be insured. As one observer noted, "Why
get involved with people where you are, when you know you'll soon
be leaving them? Why get close to anyone, when you know in
advance that making friends, close friends, only means more pain at
parting?" [1] People who move frequently feel that they do not have
enough time to develop close relationships. One person we inter-

[1] R. Keyes, *We, the Lonely People: Searching for Community* (New York: Harper &
Row, 1973), p. 22.

52

viewed said that his family had moved eighteen times in the last eighteen years. He had a close friend only once, when his family lived in the same town for two years.

Even the traditional definition of friendship may need revision. Emerson wrote, "A friend is a person with whom I may be sincere. Before him I may think aloud." Today, however, many people identify casual acquaintances as "friends." The neighbor with whom we share an occasional cocktail becomes a friend, as do fellow office workers with whom we discuss business, or perhaps even the dungaree-clad hitchhiker whom we pick up for company on a long-distance car trip.

Mobility discourages deep attachments, but the absence of intimacy may occur even in long-term relationships. Many people cautiously conceal their true feelings under the guise of being discreet. One college student described to us how she maintained an "air of mystery" to friends and acquaintances.

> I don't think it is wise to tell everything about myself to everybody, even to close friends. In almost any subject, sex, drugs, family relationships, or anything, there is something that I won't tell anybody, and I just keep it to myself. It's not that I don't trust people with information about myself, but . . . why take a chance? I just know that I know and that is enough. They can go along living without knowing things about me.

> I can imagine that someday I will meet someone whom I can tell personal things to. Right now I don't have any desire to tell anyone yet. There might be someone whom I may meet and I'll just feel like pouring everything out to him . . . but I haven't met him yet.

A fear of rejection may inhibit many people from speaking honestly about their feelings. They reason, "Why risk being hurt?" We don't have to worry about losing friends or antagonizing others when we carefully guard what we say. Chaucer stated this view succinctly in *The Canterbury Tales:* "Keep well thy tongue and keep thy friends."

There is another reason for avoiding intimacy. As we have seen, in disclosing personal information we make ourselves vulnerable. When others have access to our secrets, they acquire leverage against us. This information may be used as a weapon against us later in the relationship. We also know that divulging embarrassing information may hurt the ones we love, as many a shamefaced husband discovers after confessing to his wife about a sexual encounter with another woman.

MISS PEACH   By Mell Lazarus

Drawing by Mell Lazarus; reprinted courtesy of Mell Lazarus and Publishers-Hall Syndicate. Copyright, Field Enterprises.

In some instances it is easier to disclose intimate information to a complete stranger than to a friend, especially when further encounters are unlikely, such as on an airplane, a train, or in a hotel bar away from home. Over a hundred years ago, sociologist Georg Simmel wrote, "The stranger . . . often receives the most surprising openness—confidences which sometimes have the character of a confessional and which would be carefully withheld from a more closely related person."[2] The stranger who moves on poses no threat. He will never be in a position to use the other person's disclosure against him. Simmel observed that the stranger may be more objective in his reactions than a close friend, whose responses are biased by his feelings toward the discloser.

At times, friendship may be a barrier to intimate disclosure. Lynn Caine has described how she found it necessary to pretend to friends and to her dying husband that everything was as usual:

> I was afraid. And I was aching to talk about it. Usually I am a very private woman, but during these months I talked to people at any and every opportunity. Strangers. People for whom I wouldn't have to role-play.

[2] G. Simmel, "The Stranger," in K. H. Wolff, ed., *The Sociology of Georg Simmel* (Glencoe, Ill.: Free Press, 1950), p. 404.

I traveled a lot on my job. And on trains and planes I created every possible occasion to tell strangers, absolute strangers, that my husband was dying. One time on the shuttle to Boston, my seatmate asked, "Are you as nervous as you look? Are you afraid of flying?" He was very kind and concerned.

I found myself saying, "No, I'm not scared of flying. My husband has cancer. He's dying." [3]

THE VALUE OF FRIENDSHIP

People may alleviate their loneliness or gain fresh perspective on a problem by talking with a receptive stranger. It is easier for a person to share personal intimacies with a fellow passenger on a coast-to-coast jet flight because they will not meet again. But these encounters will not diminish for long the loneliness people feel. We need more durable relationships for that.

What is the value of an intimate friendship? Why risk being hurt by making ourselves vulnerable? There are several reasons. First, close friendships make us feel wanted and needed. Listening patiently to another's disclosures may help the other person, and it enhances our feeling of importance in the relationship. One coed reported to us that she knew her boyfriend really loved her when he shared a secret with her:

> That time I knew he really cared about me. His father had died when he was five, and he never talked about it. Even his mother said that she felt it would help him if he would talk about it. Then he told me all his memories. He got to the point of really crying. Of course he had cried before, but that time made me feel he really cared about me, and I was so glad. I can't hold anything inside, and he had been holding so much inside.

Sharing information about our problems also helps us discover that our problems are not unique. We may have an exaggerated view of our difficulties until we learn that others undergo similar experiences. An adolescent girl may worry inordinately about not having a weekend date, until she finds that many other girls *and*

[3] L. Caine, *Widow* (New York: Morrow, 1974), p. 47.

boys have the same problem. An expectant mother may be troubled by the prospect of a new child; meeting with other expectant parents can help her see that her anxieties are not unusual.

There is a third reason for sharing secrets. We often worry about doing things correctly. Are we spending enough time on studies? Should we really be dating that person? Are we happy with our careers and life styles? Talking with others about our problems may help us evaluate what we should do. Self-disclosure is a vehicle for gaining feedback and reducing uncertainty about how to behave. According to Leon Festinger's theory of social comparison, we look to "social reality." [4] Consulting with and seeking the advice of friends can help us decide an appropriate course of action. Just comparing our own experiences with theirs can help us place our problems in perspective.

Problems with dating relationships are of particular concern to young people. How to behave on dates, what to talk about, how deeply to become involved—these are matters they discuss among themselves. One coed, for instance, explained to us how she sought advice from her roommate when a boy she liked didn't kiss her on their first date. Another subject, Gail, a student in high school, described to us how she had long talks with a close girlfriend over her dating problem:

> I wanted to date this black guy that my parents wouldn't let me date. I was dating him on the side. My girlfriend, Sue, really helped me. I wanted to date him, but I had to make the decision to stop dating him. We used to sit and talk about it and just sort of analyze the situation. She was someone I could talk freely to.
>
> She told me what she thought and I respected her opinion. She had more experience with boys at that time than I did. I needed someone like that to tell me what was going on, and I couldn't talk to my parents because they would just blow up.

This young woman relied on the expertise and advice of her friend in making up her mind about dating. Unlike the parents, who could not see beyond the race issue, the friend helped Gail explore the various implications of dating the young man: How much did

[4] L. Festinger, "A Theory of Social Comparison Processes," *Human Relations*, 7 (1954), 117–40.

he really like her? How important were her parents' opinions to her? And so forth.

GETTING TO KNOW YOU

Joan M. enrolled at a large state university. She was away from home for the first time, and she shared a dormitory room with another girl. She reported to us how she got to know her friend and roommate, Janet:

> When I came on campus, I really didn't know anybody. I was pretty busy the first couple of weeks. Going to classes, buying books, learning the campus, and getting my fall schedule straight—all these things took a lot of time. My roommate had already been here for a semester, and she helped me find my way around. She pointed out the buildings to me and showed me where my classes were.
>
> In the first few days we talked about general stuff. Where we came from, what we were interested in. I really didn't know her very well then. One night, though, she and I were both studying in our room, and we got to talking about our personal lives. We had done the same things when we were younger, we had gotten into the same kinds of trouble. It was funny because our lives were kind of parallel to each other. We came from the same types of backgrounds.
>
> We talked about some pretty serious things. We were talking about our boyfriends, how they were on dope and how bad they were addicted and how we didn't want to date them anymore because of it. I think she knows me pretty well now. I can start to say something and she can just pick it right up and say what I was going to say.
>
> She tells me just about everything about herself. She wants me to go to her house to meet her family and friends. We do a lot of things together now. We go to parties together, to Zero's [a local campus hangout], and to the basketball games.

Joan's account typifies a sequence of events that can occur as two persons become more intimate. They share more personal information as they learn to trust each other. This mutual openness helps accelerate the development of a relationship, besides providing evidence of how far the relationship has moved already. As two persons become more intimate, they also become more efficient in communicating. Information is transmitted and received quickly and accurately. It isn't necessary to repeat messages. The individuals are not hiding behind masks or playing roles that they have assigned themselves; they are more sensitive in understanding each other.

Although we have emphasized the value of self-disclosure in forming relationships, an absence of openness may not necessarily reflect dissatisfaction or lack of involvement. Some individuals get along without divulging personal information, although considerable burdens are placed on them to solve their own problems.

How well do *you* know your "closest friend"? You can find out by completing the following questionnaire:

Friendship and Acquaintance as Demonstrated by a Self-disclosure Questionnaire

1. Whether or not I have ever gone to a church other than my own. (2.85)
2. The number of children I want to have after I am married. (5.91)
3. How frequently I like to engage in sexual activity. (10.02)
4. Whether I would rather live in an apartment or a house after getting married. (3.09)
5. What birth control methods I would use in marriage. (9.31)
6. What I do to attract a member of the opposite sex whom I like. (8.54)
7. How often I usually go on dates. (5.28)
8. Times that I have lied to my girlfriend (boyfriend). (8.56)
9. My feelings about discussing sex with my friends. (7.00)
10. How I might feel (or actually felt) if I saw my father hit my mother. (9.50)
11. The degree of independence and freedom from family rules which I have (had) while living at home. (5.39)
12. How often my aunts and uncles and family get together. (2.89)
13. Who my favorite relatives (e.g., aunts, uncles, etc.) are and why. (5.83)
14. How I feel about getting old. (6.36)
15. The parts of my body I am most ashamed for anyone to see. (8.88)

16. My feelings about lending money. (4.75)
17. My most pressing need for money right now (e.g., outstanding debts, some major purchase that is needed or desired). (6.88)
18. How much I spend for my clothes. (7.17)
19. Laws that I would like to see put into effect. (3.08)
20. Whether or not I ever cried as an adult when I was sad. (8.94)
21. How angry I get when people hurry me. (5.33)
22. What animals make me nervous. (3.44)
23. What it takes to hurt my feelings deeply. (9.37)
24. What I am most afraid of. (8.25)
25. How I really feel about the people I work for or with. (7.29)
26. The kinds of things I do that I don't want people to watch. (8.85)

This questionnaire measures the level of intimacy in relationships with significant persons in one's life.[5] Think of someone whom you hardly know (a casual acquaintance) and one of your closest friends. Then, for each of these target persons circle the statements that represent information you would be willing to disclose to the person in a private conversation.

After completing the questionnaire for each target person, compute two kinds of scores in the following way. One measure, *topic breadth,* is the number of statements that you circled. A second measure, *topic depth,* measures the average level of disclosure intimacy; it is computed by adding the numbers within the parentheses of the statements that were selected, and then dividing this total by the number of topic statements circled. It is likely that the breadth and depth scores will be greater for the friend than for the casual acquaintance. Such a result would support the prediction that self-disclosure is a function of the degree of relationship between individuals. If the scores did not differ by much, your definition of a close friend is not based on verbal intimacy—be-

[5] The items for the self-disclosure questionnaire were drawn from a list of statements compiled by D. A. Taylor and I. Altman, "Intimacy-Scaled Stimuli for Use in Research on Interpersonal Exchange," Naval Medical Research Institute, Tech. Report No. 9, MF 022.01.03–1002, May, 1966. See also D. A. Taylor and I. Altman, "Intimacy-Scaled Stimuli for Use in Studies of Interpersonal Relations," *Psychological Reports,* 19 (1966), 729–30.

cause you are equally open or taciturn with friends and strangers.[6]

THE DOLLARS AND CENTS OF MAKING FRIENDS

Let's follow Roger, who is going to a cocktail party in his apartment house. He walks in the door, says hello to a few friends, and then goes to the first attractive girl he sees. Roger smiles and says, "Hi, it's a nice evening for a party. There's a good group of people here. Don't you think so?" Staring over Roger's shoulder, the girl responds icily, "Really? I don't think so. I'm even sorry that I came." Roger steps back a foot or two, mumbles something about needing a drink, and excuses himself. He eases himself past a few people and approaches another attractive girl, Karen. He introduces himself and offers to get her a drink. Karen quickly smiles and accepts. Not surprisingly, Roger decides to spend more time with Karen during the evening.

Later in the evening, Roger tells Karen about the various jobs he had while attending college. He mentions his interest in cooking, and he hesitantly says that he frequently becomes nervous at a party when he is meeting others for the first time. Karen, in turn, tells Roger about the trouble she is having at school with her studies, explaining that she took too many courses this semester. She also says that she was uncomfortable about coming to the party by herself.

The case of Roger and Karen represents what might happen as two persons get to know each other. Initially, they tend to talk about superficial material: their interests, jobs, hobbies, and the weather—"small talk." Intimate information is not exchanged during this early stage of a relationship. Interaction is limited by

[6] Although we emphasize the verbal aspects of intimacy, there are nonverbal dimensions that are important. Touching, physical proximity, leaning forward, eye contact, and sharing physical possessions are just a few ways people make themselves accessible to others in a social relationship. One investigator, Albert Mehrabian, has even suggested that a person's nonverbal behavior and tone of voice have more impact than words in communicating feelings and attitudes. Thus, individuals who may be quite closed in their verbal self-disclosure may be very open nonverbally, and vice versa. See Mehrabian's *Nonverbal Communication* (Chicago: Aldine, 1972).

the roles being played—boy meeting girl, professor talking to student, or employer talking to employee. It is only after two persons decide to deepen the relationship, after spending some time together, that their self-disclosure increases.

Friendships develop as a function of a continual process of sampling and forecasting. We spend a lot of time with someone, see how enjoyable it is, and then calculate if it is worthwhile continuing the relationship. If we decide to pursue the relationship, we try to get the other person to continue too. For example, in our illustration Roger may have mentioned his nervousness at parties (which is fairly intimate information) to show Karen that he trusted and liked her. Karen may have talked about her own anxieties in order to show Roger that she liked him. The way that each person reacts to the other's disclosures indicates how the friendship will develop.

The budding relationship could have been terminated abruptly if, for instance, Karen had said to Roger, "It's dumb to get nervous about going to parties," or, worse, if she had joked about Roger's nervousness to others. If all goes well, we can expect Roger and Karen to spend more time together. Roger will probably ask Karen for a date, and both will divulge more intimate material to each other. They will gradually risk a degree of intimacy that permits each to see what the other is like and to test the strength of their relationship.

Making friends is similar to the way business executives invest money in a new company. We try to maximize the rewards and reduce the costs incurred in social encounters.[7] We try to get others to produce "rewards"—behaviors that will satisfy our needs. "Costs," on the other hand, represent the painful or negative aspects of dealing with others (for example, the threat of rejection, the loss of esteem, or boredom), which reduce our motivation to continue knowing someone.

Self-disclosure plays a vital role in understanding the process of friendship formation. Besides providing an index of the degree of

---

[7] J. W. Thibaut and H. H. Kelley, *The Social Psychology of Groups* (New York: John Wiley, 1959); and G. C. Homans, *Social Behavior: Its Elementary Forms* (New York: Harcourt, Brace and World, 1961).

closeness in a relationship, self-disclosure functions as a direct reward or cost in social encounters. We evaluate others according to how much they help us with our problems, whether they care for what we say, and whether they are willing to trust us enough to share with us their personal problems or secret thoughts.

We have emphasized how individuals tend to be guarded in their disclosures as they test each other. Persons stick close to role-defined behaviors or focus on their positive attributes in order to avoid rejection. If a relationship is to develop, however, the individuals must take the risk of being honest about their feelings.

Wallace Hamilton, a New York-based writer, described how candor can increase closeness between people:[8] Lamont Courtney Bostwick, a male homosexual, claims to have been born in Ethiopia, where his family owns a major passenger airline. His wealthy grandmother supposedly lives in New York. He also claims to be a professional dancer. Several persons, including Hamilton, doubt Lamont's story and suspect that he has stolen clothes and money from them. Lamont lamely pleads innocent, but then breaks down to tell his real story. His real name is Andy Jones, and his home is a farm near Athens, Georgia. Lamont confesses, "When I was fourteen, they [the family] sent me to live with my grandmother up in Harlem. I started hanging around the Village. I met guys, and they made love to me, and I like that. They took care of me, too." Hamilton asks Lamont, "What's all this thing about Ethiopia?" Lamont replies, "Who wants a black boy from Georgia? . . . So I made it up." Here is Hamilton's reaction to Lamont's honesty: "I held him for a very long time, and he held me. I went through some heavy changes. Who wants a black boy from Georgia? I sure as hell did, and a lot more than I wanted some gilded youth from the other side of the world. Somehow, Lamont had come home as Andy Jones. . . . 'I like Andy Jones just fine,' I said."

This illustration shows how self-disclosure may speed up intimacy. The aspects of ourselves that we hide may actually improve the chances of a successful relationship if we reveal them.

[8] W. Hamilton, *Christopher and Gay* (New York: Saturday Review Press, 1973), pp. 47–48.

Individuals undoubtedly differ in the rate and pattern of their self-disclosures. In the next section, we will examine the various levels of intimacy that individuals maintain in their relationships.

SOCIAL PENETRATION THEORY

How do people decide what information to reveal about themselves? Do people differ in the kinds of information they reveal? Do reward-cost calculations affect strategies of self-disclosure? Social penetration theory, developed by Irwin Altman and Dalmas Taylor, provides a useful framework for examining patterns of self-disclosure in a relationship.[9] According to social penetration theory, individuals generally disclose more information as a relationship progresses to more intimate levels. They will talk more intimately, disclose information about an increasing number of areas, and within each area they will disclose more pieces of information and dwell on them for a longer time.

These stages may be represented as a series of "wedges" being driven into one's personality. Figure 4–1 is an example of the wedge-shaped nature of disclosure. At each stage of relationship more information is disclosed at superficial than at intimate levels; thus, breadth of disclosure decreases as a function of the depth (or intimacy) of the conversation. As the relationship between individuals advances—from strangers to casual acquaintances to close friends—disclosure expands on both the breadth and depth dimensions. The wedge therefore widens and deepens. The individuals exchange more information and at greater levels of intimacy. Studies of dormitory roommates[10] and men who live together in isolation[11] indicate that this pattern of disclosure occurs regularly.

Two important aspects of Figure 4–1 should be noted. First, disclosure in some areas may remain at the same level of intimacy

[9] I. Altman and D. A. Taylor, *Social Penetration: The Development of Interpersonal Relationships* (New York: Holt, Rinehart and Winston, 1970).

[10] D. A. Taylor, "The Development of Interpersonal Relationships: Social Penetration Processes," *Journal of Social Psychology*, 75 (1968), 79–90.

[11] I. Altman and D. A. Taylor, "Interpersonal Exchange in Isolation," *Sociometry*, 28 (1965), 411–26.

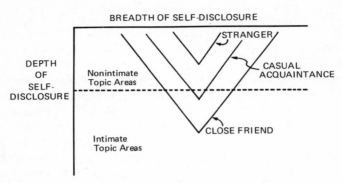

Figure 4–1 Breadth and depth of self-disclosure at three stages of a relationship. (Adapted from I. Altman and W. W. Haythorn, "Interpersonal Exchange in Isolation," *Sociometry*, 28 (1965), Figure 3, p. 422.)

as the relationship develops. If individuals enjoy talking at certain levels of intimacy about sports, hobbies, or other common interests, disclosure will continue at these levels in the future, even though it may become deeper in other topics. Second, disclosure proceeds gradually into more intimate areas, primarily because of the greater potential for embarrassment in these areas. Persons who move too quickly into intimate levels of disclosure may suffer crises if unexpected costs arise. For instance, new roommates may be very open with each other and subsequently find out that the information disclosed has been used to ridicule them. Our prospects of being hurt are reduced when we carefully gauge the effects of disclosure at each level of intimacy.[12]

[12] The reader may ask, "How does one know when a person is talking intimately, or that depth of disclosure is very great?" Judgments about intimacy are basically subjective. There are no absolute standards for deciding when a person is communicating intimately or nonintimately. In our own research, though, we have been able to achieve moderate to high levels of agreement on this point, suggesting that judges can rate intimacy without too much difficulty.

Though much research still needs to be done, there are at least two factors that affect ratings of intimacy. First, disclosure that reveals unique information about a

An example of the developmental changes in self-disclosure was reported by Dalmas Taylor in a longitudinal study.[13] Fifteen pairs of college roommates, who were not acquainted initially, were studied for one semester in dormitories at the University of Delaware. During the first, third, sixth, ninth, and thirteenth weeks of the semester, two types of self-disclosure measures were administered. One questionnaire inquired about the sorts of activities roommates had shared during the preceding three weeks. The second questionnaire asked subjects to indicate whether they had revealed information about themselves to their roommates in each of forty content areas (such as religion and family). Supporting the concept of disclosure as wedgelike, breadth of self-disclosure tended to be greater for superficial material than for intimate material. In both superficial and intimate areas of exchange, self-disclosure increased in depth as a function of the number of weeks that the roommates had known each other. There was also a tendency for breadth of disclosure to increase at a faster rate for superficial areas of disclosure.

Besides the wedge shape, there are other possible patterns of disclosure in an intimate relationship. In a summer romance, persons tend to disclose highly intimate information about themselves in very limited areas. Breadth of disclosure is approximately the same at every level of intimacy. These relationships are likely to be very fragile and short-lived. There are several different areas in which the individuals have not built up a working relationship with each other. Subsequent disclosure of intimate information that is unacceptable to the other person may precipitate a quick end to the relationship.

Imagine a young couple who fall in love during a weekend

---

person is usually more intimate than disclosure that does not. For example, information about one's birthplace may have a lower intimacy rating than information about one's personal attitudes. Explaining where you spent your time in the army is less intimate than describing how you spent your time in a particular place. Second, information about feelings or behavior that we would not want most people to know is more intimate than information that we don't mind telling publicly. The more vulnerable that information about ourselves will make us, the less likely we are to reveal it.

[13] Taylor, "The Development of Interpersonal Relationships."

holiday at a mountain resort. They talk enthusiastically about their common interests, setting up an apartment, beginning a new life together, even having children. However, the romance quickly crumbles when she attempts to explain an abortion she has had. The young man could have regarded the girl's honesty as a basis for loving her even more, for she trusted him with a closely guarded secret. However, the young man's negative reaction to the abortion proved costly. The relationship, and particularly the young man's love for the girl, was not strong enough to absorb this disturbing information.

Another possibility in such an infatuation is disenchantment as the breadth of disclosure increases. A couple who have exchanged intimate information very quickly may later find, to their dismay, that each has habits, attitudes, and eccentricities that annoy the other. She may realize, belatedly, that he brags about his money too often; he may discover that she is much more interested in being physically comfortable than in his hobby, camping in the wilderness. Such discoveries may lead to a painful termination of the relationship.

As individuals become deeply committed, they can divulge personal information that would destroy a more tenuous relationship. They develop a basis of trust that makes it easier for them to express feelings of anger and frustration honestly. Hiding behind a façade shouldn't be necessary because approval and mutual respect have been established over a long period. Now they can communicate openly about the conflicts that are inevitable in any relationship. Here is a statement by a Lesbian about being honest with her feelings about her lover.

> Being buddies gives us the freedom to blow up at each other. We know that underneath our anger we both feel a long-term commitment to each other. So we know we can yell and scream at each other without worrying "Maybe she'll get so mad she'll walk out and never come back," as we would with other people. We can show our weaknesses and our bad points to each other as well as our good points. We can be ourselves with each other.[14]

---

[14] Boston Women's Health Collective, *Our Bodies, Ourselves* (New York: Simon and Schuster, Touchstone/Clarion, 1972), p. 69.

Usually, self-disclosure increases gradually over the various stages of a relationship. However, exceptions occur. Disclosure may vary at different rates, depending upon the nature of the material being talked about. For instance, certain topics may be considered taboo even among close friends. A Protestant and a Catholic who are otherwise very close may be unable to talk with each other about abortion. The topic is highly emotional, and discussion tends to lead to controversy and bitterness. For similar reasons, husbands and wives may tacitly agree not to discuss their sexual experiences before marriage. Even relatively superficial topics may be off limits because of a lack of common interest.

In a relationship, disclosure is likely to increase particularly in those areas in which both individuals feel comfortable talking. In a number of areas, similarity of interest is a prerequisite for mutual self-disclosure. True friends, though, might be able to take an interest in whatever interests the other person simply because they care about each other. On the other hand, it is easier for someone to say to a close friend than to an acquaintance, "Hey, you know I'm really not interested in that subject."

Breaking Up

Just as relationships can progress into more intimate areas, a reversal of this process can occur. In the latter case, the relationship produces fewer rewards for the individuals and a possible increase in the costs incurred by continued interaction. One of our subjects described to us a harsh example of this process. She told her mother that she had an abortion. Her mother said that she wanted nothing more to do with her, so the girl left home and got her own apartment. The girl's disclosure about her abortion ended the relationship.

Other kinds of experiences may make it fruitless to continue a relationship. Two persons may discover that their personality styles conflict; for instance, they may both want to dominate the relationship. In other cases, a person likes someone very much but finds out that the other individual doesn't want to become intimate. One subject told us that he liked his girl friend a lot, but she balked at becoming too intimate. This is the way he described the rise and fall of his relationship with her:

> At the beginning we got along really well. We seemed to fit together. We enjoyed the same things. We would go to concerts together, and we would talk about that. We had the same interests. It was easy for me to talk to her.
>
> As we got to know one another, she would be open to a certain extent, but she knew she had this problem about being closed or standoffish from people. There are some things she keeps inside and she doesn't tell anyone, such as personal problems she had in dating relationships. She kept some of her feelings inside, so I never was completely sure how she felt towards me. It was really frustrating because I didn't know whether she really liked me enough [for me] to keep on dating her. I finally told her that I really liked her, and she said that she was just fond of me. Then we knew that either she would have to start liking me or we might as well forget about it. So that was what we did . . . Sometimes, I still see her around campus and we say hello.

The deterioration process is often comparable to a film being shown in reverse; a gradual decrease occurs in breadth and depth of exchange of information. Disclosure returns to more superficial areas, where the costs connected with further interaction are slight. The person who experiences an unfavorable reward/cost ratio may decide, "Why should I take a chance and trust him any more with my personal feelings? I am only going to get hurt." The reversal in self-disclosure processes will continue until the individuals have found a mutually acceptable level of exchange. Former lovers may find it suitable to be "just good friends." In other cases, where the rewards have become so meager and the costs so great, the individuals may want to have nothing further to do with each other.

How Many Friends Are Enough?

Is one intimate person, perhaps a spouse or a lover, sufficient? Do we need more close friends than that to obtain the values connected with openness?

Some individuals argue that we should be completely honest

with everyone. For instance, leaders in the encounter and communal movements believe that open communication is essential for successful relationships. They argue that "if we hide information about ourself to someone, we are treating him like an object. We are managing our impression so that we can pull strings in the relationship." One psychotherapist calls this phenomenon of considering persons as machines or objects "thinging." [15] Hiding behind a mask, we consider others only in terms of their function, role, or utilitarian value. Thus, the gasoline attendant is merely an extension of the machine that fills the tank.

It seems necessary for us to limit the number of intimate associates we maintain. We wouldn't have the time or energy to cultivate any close and intimate relationships if everyone made a claim to our friendship. Little empirical research exists about the effects of the number of intimate friends on one's degree of psychological adjustment. However, Harvey Cox has persuasively argued the case of limiting friendships.

> He [urban man] must have more or less impersonal relationships with most of the people with whom he comes in contact precisely in order to choose certain friendships to nourish and cultivate. This selectivity can be symbolized perhaps by the unplugged telephone or the unlisted number. A person does not request an unlisted number to cut down on the depth of his relationships. Quite the opposite; he does so to guard and deepen the worthwhile relationships he has against being dissolved in the deluge of messages that would come if one were open on principle and on an equal basis to anyone who tried to get through. . . . Those we want to know have our number; others do not: We are free to use the switchboard without being victimized by its infinite possibilities.[16]

We must maintain different levels of social distance with the various people we meet every day. By limiting contact with most of the people we see, we have time for deep relationships with just a few individuals with whom we wish to be close.

In this chapter we have noted how self-disclosure changes over the different stages of a relationship. Though intimacy may be

[15] G. R. Bach and R. M. Deutsch, *Pairing* (New York: Peter H. Wyden, 1970).
[16] H. Cox, *The Secular City* (New York: Macmillan, 1965), p. 41.

difficult, involving the risk of occasional embarrassment or ridicule, it substantially improves our opportunity for getting close to others. Making ourselves known to others shows them that we trust them and, in turn, that they can trust us. Problems of loneliness and isolation will only be overcome as people move beyond casual, superficial encounters.

Next, we will examine the role of self-disclosure in marriage. What is the value of intimacy when persons interact with each other on a day-to-day basis?

intimacy in marriage

> One rule of thumb which I have found helpful for
> myself is that in any continuing relationship, any
> persistent feeling had better be expressed. Suppressing it
> can only damage the relationship. The first sentence is
> not stated casually. Only if it is a significant continuing
> relationship, and only if it is a recurring or persistent
> feeling, is it necessary to bring the feeling into the open
> in the relationship. If this is not done, what is
> unexpressed gradually poisons the relationship . . .
>
> —Carl Rogers

Self-disclosure seems necessary in establishing and maintaining deep interpersonal relationships. For most adult Americans, marriage is the relationship in which the highest levels of disclosure are expected. The spouse serves the role of confidant and best friend, someone whom we can trust more than anyone else. The ability to share intimacies attests to the closeness of the couple. The partners' ability to divulge personal and even potentially embarrassing material—without fear and threat—demonstrates their respect and affection for each other. A person whom we interviewed recalled that he felt depressed over a "poor performance" at a public speaking function. Talking to his wife, explaining what had happened, and having her say that she sympathized made the experience bearable.

Sometimes, withholding feelings can benefit the relationship. Nondisclosure may be the best solution, particularly if the disclosure would be perceived as threatening or punitive. However, a pattern of deception in an otherwise intimate relationship can be dangerous in the long run. Such a pattern raises questions about the reason for the façade and whether the relationship is, in fact, worth maintaining. A young woman we interviewed described how her husband's deceit made her feel that she could not trust him.

> My husband was in the navy, and he went out to sea. He got paid while he was out at sea, and he spent his whole pay check while he was gone. He then borrowed money so that when he got home I wouldn't know that he had spent his whole pay check. I began to notice ten and fifteen dollars, which we didn't even have to spare, disappearing from the pay checks, evidently to pay back the money he had borrowed. I questioned him about it and he did confess. He said that he borrowed the money to show me that he had some money when he came home. I said, "Look, what's going on? You lied to me. And if you lie to me, I can't trust you. And if I can't trust you, I can't respect you, and if I can't respect you, I can't love you. That's a destructive thing, to lie." And he thought that it was a real funny matter. He just shrugged it off, like what's the big deal. "I am sure," he said, "that you have lied in your life. Probably it wasn't the last lie that I will tell, so don't get uptight about it."

LOVE—BEING ABLE TO CONFIDE

Many psychologists, including Carl Rogers and Sidney Jourard, hold that self-disclosure is a prerequisite for developing an intimate "love" relationship such as marriage. Jourard suggests that an inability to disclose precludes the capacity to love:

> A self-alienated person—one who does not disclose himself truthfully and fully—can never love another person nor can he be loved by the other person. Effective loving calls for knowledge of the object. How can I love a person whom I do not know? How can the person love me if he does not know me? [1]

This statement casts a rather harsh indictment on marriages that are not based on psychological intimacy. However, many marriages are quite successful despite an absence of high mutual disclosure. Sexual adjustment, economic security, and outside interests may make a "distant" relationship tolerable if not deeply satisfying. Nevertheless, most research indicates, with a few exceptions to be discussed in the next section, that self-disclosure is positively

---

[1] S. Jourard, *The Transparent Self* (Princeton, N.J.: Van Nostrand, 1964), p. 25.

related to deep emotional attachment and marital satisfaction.[2]

George Levinger and David Senn asked each partner of thirty-two couples in metropolitan Cleveland, Ohio to complete self-disclosure and marital-satisfaction questionnaires.[3] The self-disclosure questionnaire asked the subject to indicate the proportion of feelings that he divulged to his partner in each of nine areas of communication (handling family money, sex relations, work, own parents, spouse's parents, and so forth). Subjects also estimated how much their spouse had divulged in each area. Each person was also asked to indicate how favorably he felt about disclosure in each area. Thus, a measure could be derived of the extent of disclosure of *pleasant* as opposed to *unpleasant* feelings to the spouse.

The results indicated a positive relationship between marital satisfaction and disclosure of feelings to one's spouse. Couples who reported disclosing a higher proportion of feelings to each other had happier marriages. Interestingly, marital satisfaction correlated more highly with disclosure of pleasant feelings than with disclosure of unpleasant feelings. "Spilling out everything" was not as useful in the marital relationship as a selective disclosure of feelings. A response bias may exist in these results, however: some people may not admit to having unpleasant feelings or to being dissatisfied.

Zick Rubin has conducted fascinating studies on the nature of romantic love.[4] He has constructed a "love scale," of which self-disclosure is an important component. This scale is composed of three primary factors: *intimacy,* or self-disclosure ("I feel that I can confide in ——— about virtually everything"); *attachment* ("If I were lonely, my first thought would be to seek ——— out"); and

---

[2] See R. O. Blood, Jr. and D. M. Wolfe, *Husbands and Wives: The Dynamics of Married Living* (Glencoe, Ill.: Free Press, 1960); M. Komarovsky, *Blue-Collar Marriage* (New York: Random House, Vintage, 1967); and P. C. Pineo, "Disenchantment in the Later Years of Marriage," *Marriage and Family Living,* 23 (1961), 3–11.

[3] G. Levinger and D. J. Senn, "Disclosure of Feelings in Marriage," *Merrill-Palmer Quarterly of Behavior and Development,* 13 (1967), 237–49.

[4] Z. Rubin, *Liking and Loving: An Invitation to Social Psychology* (New York: Holt, Rinehart and Winston, 1973); see especially Chapter 10. Or see Rubin, "Liking and Loving," in Z. Rubin, ed., *Doing Unto Others* (Englewood Cliffs, N.J.: Prentice-Hall, 1975).

caring ("I would do almost anything for ——— "). The love scale scores correlate highly with individuals' estimates of how likely they are to disclose personal information and to marry their current dating partners.

Though correlational studies indicate that self-disclosure is positively related to marital satisfaction, the causality almost certainly operates in both directions: high self-disclosure may increase marital harmony, but marital harmony may produce high self-disclosure.

WEIGHING THE CONSEQUENCES OF DISCLOSURE

There may be exceptions to the generalization that self-disclosure is positively related to marital satisfaction. Even when the apparent intent of the discloser may be to encourage honesty and openness in the relationship, complications may occur which should have been considered in advance. A marriage counselor whom we interviewed described one such case:

> A couple came in for counseling. One of the husband's problems was that he did not feel sexually adequate. His wife had described to him what she had done in her relationship with another man, things that he had never thought of doing himself. Hearing these things made him feel even less adequate, so that he pulled back further and further from her. They couldn't reestablish any kind of a satisfactory sexual relationship because he was always trying to live up to her standards.

A study by Beverly Cutler and William Dyer of Brigham Young University explored the effects of a couple's willingness to discuss disagreements about marital adjustment.[5] They found that when one spouse attempted to share the feeling that the partner had violated some marital expectancy (for instance, about household expenses or taking care of the house), the results included pouting, getting upset, and emotional outbursts. Many spouses couldn't cope with hearing negative information about themselves. The authors'

[5] B. R. Cutler and W. G. Dyer, "Initial Adjustment Processes in Young Married Couples," *Social Forces,* 44 (1965), 195–201.

main conclusion emphasizes the need to examine the impact of the disclosure on the partner. Here are some illustrations of errors in judgment that an indiscreet discloser might make:

1. The statement, "You are spending too much money on your clothes," may be interpreted as a put-down. The target person may think, "What he is really trying to say is that I can't handle money and that he doesn't trust me."
2. The timing of the disclosure may be inappropriate. How many times have spouses brought up important matters when their partner is exhausted after a busy day at home or in the office?
3. Certain disclosures may be threatening, and their impact should be considered in advance. Informing your partner that your mutual sexual relations are inadequate may undermine a weak personality, producing a defensive reaction such as, "It's not me, but you who has the problem!"
4. Certain material may be perceived as inappropriate to discuss. A wife might complain that her husband has no business questioning her about her premarital sexual activities.

There are other reasons for withholding information from one's partner. The information might be used subsequently as ammunition in a quarrel. One of the students we interviewed mentioned how his wife had once confided to him information about her father's extramarital affair, which, told to her mother, would have destroyed her parents' marriage. Currently involved in a bitter divorce proceeding, he reported threatening to divulge this information if his wife demanded an "unrealistic" divorce settlement.

It should be noted that in most marriages, self-disclosure is usually reciprocal.[6] Both individuals have disclosed information at a similar level of intimacy. Thus, the partners are safeguarded from blackmail because each knows information about the other; this deters the betrayal of confidences. To illustrate, a man in his mid-twenties might tell his fiancée that he is still a virgin. In turn, she might trust him with some little-known but embarrassing information about herself. If their relationship deteriorates, each person may avoid ridiculing the other because of the potentially damaging material they both know.

[6] This is indicated in the studies by Levinger and Senn, *op. cit.* and Komarovsky, *op. cit.*

For some individuals, hearing intimate disclosures is a burden. As folksinger Carly Simon wrote in the song, "We Have No Secrets," some persons may not want to know everything about their lover's past:

> *Sometimes I wish*
> *Often I wish*
> *That I never knew*
> *Some of those secrets of yours.*[7]

The discussion in this section may leave the impression that hiding feelings is beneficial. Nondisclosure may provide some temporary advantage, but it is doubtful that this procedure is worthwhile in the long run. Negative feelings that are not disclosed in some manner may accumulate and assume exaggerated importance over time. A young woman who planned to marry her boyfriend within a few months described to us a problem of this kind:

David sometimes does things that really bug me. The first time he might do it, I'll say to myself, "Well, forget about it." For instance, he once said in front of a lot of people that I talk a lot, that I have a big mouth; and that bothered and embarrassed me. I said to myself, "This time I will forgive him." Then he did it again, and I didn't like it. Then he did it a third time, and I said something and we got in an argument. The first two times I just let it build up over a period of a month or two. I had a tremendous resentment towards him and he didn't even know it. It affected me so that I was much colder with him. Things seemed to be going sour. I moped around and I wasn't very friendly. He knew I was moping, but he had no idea why. When it finally came out, he said, "What are you talking about? That happened two months ago! I thought that was such a little thing."

George Bach and Peter Wyden describe this phenomenon as "gunny sacking": " . . . complaints are toted along quietly in a gunny sack for any length of time . . . [and then] make a dreadful

---

[7] WE HAVE NO SECRETS, Copyright © 1972 by Quackenbush Music, Ltd. Used by permission of Quackenbush Music, Ltd.

mess when the sack finally bursts." [8] A recent study of married couples in the Washington, D.C. metropolitan area confirms Bach and Wyden's speculations about gunny sacking.[9] Men who were relatively dissatisfied with their marriages tended to avoid confrontations over minor disagreements. Instead, they did not reveal their feelings until their marriages were threatened by a serious problem. Often, the ensuing argument led to the couple's estrangement.

Richard Lessor has imaginatively described the eventual effect of withholding feelings about disagreements:

. . . some partners in marriage treat punishments like trading stamps. They put them away and save them for something really big. Some people choose not to express their emotions spontaneously, so they set up an elaborate system of storing them. The punishments can be saved or traded. A number of small slights—each worth "X"—can be saved until "25 X" punishment can be delivered. Wow! [10]

BARRIERS TO DISCLOSURE IN MARRIAGE [11]

Though self-disclosure may be desirable in sustaining an intimate relationship, cultural factors prevent many couples from knowing how or what to communicate to each other. Different emphasis seems to be placed on self-disclosure in lower-class families than in middle-class families. There is also plenty of evidence that men are discouraged from disclosing personal feelings, creating problems in their relationships with their wives.

Mirra Komarovsky's book, *Blue-Collar Marriage*, includes an interesting example of how self-disclosure is affected by the education of the respondents. Komarovsky asked husbands and wives to comment on stories involving communication between

[8] G. R. Bach and P. Wyden, *The Intimate Enemy: How to Fight Fair in Love and Marriage* (New York: Avon, 1970), p. 19.

[9] H. K. Raush et al., *Communication, Conflict, and Marriage* (San Francisco: Jossey-Bass, 1974).

[10] R. Lessor, *Love and Marriage and Trading Stamps: On the Care and Feeding of Marriages* (Chicago: Argus Communications, 1971), p. 96.

[11] This section is based largely on material in Chapter 3 of Komarovsky, *op. cit.* All quotations in this section are from the book (used by permission of Random House, Inc.).

partners in hypothetical married couples. Couples' responses were expected to provide information about the value they placed on sharing feelings in a marriage. Here is one of the stories used. It reflects the theme that a marriage might be in trouble because the spouses do not communicate.

> A couple has been married for seven years. The wife says that her husband is a good provider and a good man, but still she complains to her mother about her marriage. She says he comes home, reads the paper, watches T.V., but doesn't talk to her. He says he "doesn't like to gab just for the sake of talking." But she says he is not companionable and has nothing to say to her. *What do you think of this couple?*

When reactions to this study were considered in terms of the amount of education of those interviewed, better-educated couples (both spouses graduated from high school) emphasized the importance of self-disclosure between spouses. Fifty-nine percent of the high school graduates felt that the absence of conversation in this story was a problem for the couple, but only 26 percent of the less-educated couples expressed the same view.

Typical reactions of well-educated couples to this story include:

> A 31-year-old wife: She should make it interesting enough around the house to get him away from the T.V. and the newspaper; invite people over or find some things like church work or hobbies that they can work at together.

> A 25-year-old husband: He should listen to her and talk to her. He can't expect her to sit in the house all day and do her job and not have anyone to talk to at night.

Such respondents note that the marriage is in trouble and occasionally suggest possible solutions for the wife's dilemma.

The less-educated couples often noted that the wife had no legitimate grievance; they felt that if the husband wanted to be left alone, that was his business. Here are some typical reactions from this group.

> A 28-year-old wife: Gee, can you tie that? He's generous, don't bother her, he just keeps out of the way, and she's fussing and wants him to sit there and entertain her.

A 38-year-old construction worker: If you do right by a woman and your job, they owe you a little rest to yourself.

The different norms held by the two groups about the appropriateness of self-disclosure were reflected in their own self-disclosure patterns. Interviewees were asked to what extent they disclosed their "emotional concerns" (about children, marriage, and work) to their spouse. The results indicated that the high school graduates disclosed more personal information to one another than did the non–high school graduates. Sixty-five percent of the more educated and only 36 percent of the less educated could be rated as engaging in "full" or "very full" communication. Only 12 percent of the better educated were rated as having "meager" or "very meager" communication, whereas 41 percent of the non–high school graduates fell into these categories.

There is a disturbing aspect to these results. Couples who have learned from their parents' example to minimize the value of communication may be unable to cope with problems that emerge in marriage and other important interpersonal relationships. The individual who won't disclose may be unable to exchange feelings and opinions in the future. Thus, the educational differences that Komarovsky found to influence the amount of self-disclosure also influenced the techniques used by couples to handle disagreements. Talking out disagreements was more frequent among the better educated, whereas violent quarreling (including name calling, shouting, and occasional physical attacks) was more frequent among the less educated.

Komarovsky did find a few couples for whom the absence of disclosure did not pose a problem. Such individuals might share personal feelings with other friends and relatives instead of with their spouses. The norm that a spouse should be one's most intimate friend was not upheld in these cases. The partners accepted psychological distance, expecting that any intimacy needs could be satisfied elsewhere. The case of Mrs. Green illustrates:

> Mrs. G sees her sister and her mother daily. "Oh yes," she said about her sister. "We tell each other everything, anything we have on our minds. We don't hold nothing back." But when asked whether she can talk to her husband, she answered: "Sure, I can talk to him

about anything that has to be said." Her view is that "men and women do different things; he don't want to be bothered with my job and I don't want to be bothered with his. Sometimes we got to do the same things, something around the house, and we have to tell each other."

THE INEXPRESSIVE MALE

Komarovsky made another important finding about couples' self-disclosure. The wives were more interested in communicating personal feelings than the husbands. Furthermore, the husbands seemed less interested—almost indifferent—to what their wives said. Here is a graphic illustration of the feelings of a woman whose husband does not care to listen:

> Not listening is probably the commonest unkindness of married life, and one that creates—more devastatingly than an eternity of forgotten birthdays and misguided Christmas gifts—an atmosphere of not loving. For if a husband tunes us out and doesn't hear us, if he doesn't want to know what's on our mind, he sets off a chilling logic that goes like this: He isn't interested, which means I'm not interesting, which means I'm unlovable, which means I'm unloved.[12]

The inability of husbands to listen is related to an overall difficulty men have in sharing personal feelings. Men are lower revealers than women,[13] and they can be perfectly satisfied with this fact. In *Blue-Collar Marriage,* for instance, more wives than husbands stressed the therapeutic value of talking about problems. Here is an illustration from an interview with a thirty-year-old woman:

> Lots of people say it's not good to go around shooting off your lips about what's eating [you], but I think the good thing is to talk it out and get it out of your system. But I have to leave him alone because if I try to get him to talk he'll get really sore, or he'll go off the deep end and walk out of here . . . . He is strictly hands-off if something

[12] J. Viorst, *Yes, Married: A Saga of Love and Complaint* (New York: Saturday Review Press, 1972), p. 148.

[13] P. C. Cozby, "Self-Disclosure: A Literature Review," *Psychological Bulletin*, 79 (1973), 73–91.

hurts him . . . . It makes it rough . . . not knowing what's eating him hurts you worse than it hurts him.[14]

Numerous problems may arise due to different expectations by men and women about how much should be disclosed. First, wives may interpret their husbands' reticence as an absence of affection. This explanation, the social attraction position, was discussed briefly in Chapter Three. The exchange of intimate information is supposed to occur between close friends; thus, the absence of disclosure by the husband may lead his mate to infer that she is not liked. Second, wives may perceive an inequity in the relationship if they disclose more about themselves than their husbands do. A norm of reciprocity underlies much of our social behavior: we feel obligated to return services that we have received. The recipient of high disclosure who fails to reciprocate puts himself and the other person into an inequitable relationship. Thus, the husband who does not reciprocate disclosure may, in his wife's view, be violating the reciprocity norm; as a result, the wife may resent the husband.

The inability of men to disclose their feelings is in part due to the different sex roles that men and women are expected to play. Men are encouraged to hide their real feelings from others as well as from themselves, and this creates barriers to effective communication in marriage and other relationships. According to Jourard, "The male role . . . will not allow man to acknowledge or to disclose the entire breadth and depth of his inner experience to himself or to others. Man seems obliged, rather, to hide much of his real self . . . ."[15]

The roots of these different sex roles can be found in childhood. Little boys are usually praised and rewarded for mastery at games and sports, whereas little girls are rewarded for their success in relationships with others. Boys are expected to be "little soldiers," who hide their feelings because "big boys don't cry." In contrast, girls are not expected to be "strong and silent"; they are allowed and even encouraged to show their feelings and emotions. Such childhood conditioning is difficult to overcome.

[14] Komarovsky, *op. cit.,* p. 156.

[15] S. Jourard, *The Transparent Self,* 2nd ed. (New York: Van Nostrand Reinhold, 1971), p. 35.

Some men are painfully aware of their inability to communicate their feelings, especially feelings that carry connotations of weakness:

Can you imagine men talking to each other saying: "Are you sure you're not angry at me?" . . . "I'm not as assertive as I would like to be." . . . "I feel so competitive that I can't get close to anyone." . . . "I just learned something important about myself that I've got to tell you." . . . "I don't have the self-confidence to do what I really want to do." . . . "I feel nervous talking to you like this."

It just doesn't happen.

. . . We are taught not to communicate our personal feelings and concerns. Most of our friendships simply don't run very deep. For example, looking back, I realize that my only points of contact with one of my closest friends of several years ago were playing poker and tennis together, eating dinners cooked by his wife, and rehashing the Vietnam war and other "large" problems. . . .

We always needed an excuse to talk. Getting together for its own sake would have been frightening. Talking personally and spontaneously involves revealing doubts, plans which may fail, ideas which haven't been thought through, happiness over things the other person may think trivial—in short, making ourselves vulnerable. That was too risky.[16]

WHEN WOMEN DON'T DISCLOSE

The sex role of the "strong and silent" man promotes low disclosure in males, but women's self-disclosure about certain areas is also inhibited by the roles expected of them. Matina Horner, president of Radcliffe College, found that many women are inhibited by a "motive to avoid success." [17] Many women are apprehensive about being rejected, losing friends, or becoming ineligible as dating or marital partners if they succeed in traditionally male-dominated fields. Thus, many women reevaluate their goals and exhaust their

[16] M. Fasteau, "Men: Why Aren't We Talking?" Ms. (July, 1972), 16; reprinted in J. Pleck and J. Sawyer, eds., Men and Masculinity (Englewood Cliffs, N.J.: Prentice-Hall, 1974).

[17] M. S. Horner, "Toward an Understanding of Achievement-Related Conflicts in Women," Journal of Social Issues, 28 (1972), 157–75.

energies in the quest for a husband or some occupation "appropriate" for women.

Besides fearing success, many women hide certain information about themselves so as not to appear threatening to their boyfriends. In a classic study conducted by Komarovsky in the 1940s, she found that approximately 40 percent of a group of female college students reported they had occasionally "played dumb" on dates. That is, the girl "concealed some academic honor, pretended ignorance of some subject, or allowed the man the last word in an intellectual discussion." Here are descriptions given by three girls of how they downgraded their own achievements:

> I am better in math than my fiancé. But while I let him explain politics to me, we never talk about math even though, being a math major, I could tell him some interesting things.

> When a girl asks me what marks I got last semester I answer, "Not so good—only one 'A' "; when a boy asks the same question, I say very brightly with a note of surprise, "Imagine, I got an 'A'!"

> Once I went sailing with a man who so obviously enjoyed the role of a protector that I told him I didn't know how to sail. As it turned out he didn't either. We got into a tough spot, and I was torn between a desire to get a hold of the boat and a fear to reveal that I had lied to him.[18]

The above transcripts were written nearly thirty years ago. Questionnaires completed in 1970 and 1971 by college women indicate a substantial drop in the percentage of those who deliberately downgrade their intellectual ability in favor of a man. Pretending to be intellectually inferior to a man still occurs occasionally, but not nearly as often as in past years.[19]

In many cases, apprehensions about the husband's or boyfriend's reactions still cause women to lower their career aspirations. Women who do succeed in areas traditionally masculine may find their relationships with men threatened. For instance, one subject we interviewed described how her marriage deteriorated after she returned to college to continue her education:

[18] M. Komarovsky, "Cultural Contradictions and Sex Roles," *American Journal of Sociology,* 52 (1946), 184–89.

[19] M. Komarovsky, "Cultural Contradictions and Sex Roles: The Masculine Case," *American Journal of Sociology,* 78 (1974), 873–84.

At first, my husband acted really glad that I was in school. It was an accomplishment. But he also thought that I would flunk out, and I think this is what kept him going. When I didn't he started getting upset . . . . Eventually, I just kept my mouth shut about what was going on at school. If I got good grades, fine, I wouldn't say a word about it. If I got bad grades, I wouldn't tell him either. We just cut off all communication about school.

Recently, consciousness raising (C–R) groups have developed in which women explore what it means to be human and female in our society. A wide range of topics are discussed. One C–R group member described that her group "spoke about husbands, lovers, privacy, sex, loneliness, role-playing in the home, our children, our parents, our housekeeping hangups, and our daily routines." [20] These groups provide an opportunity for women to take a good look at themselves and to examine the illogical demands made on them by society. Through mutual support in the C–R group, the women help one another enhance their self-image and grow as persons.

Unfortunately, both sexes are caught up in role stereotypes that need to be reevaluated. Just as many women resent the passive, dependent role attributed to them, many men resent the breadwinning, "strong-and-silent" role attributed to them. In fact, C–R groups are being formed in which men can assess their masculine image. Hopefully, these groups can provide the basis for expanding communication between the sexes without the interference of role stereotypes. As one experienced leader of men's C–R groups has said, "To the extent that a men's group helps us counter our emotional constipation, and to the extent it encourages a non-defensive openness, it establishes a basis for a communicative relationship between the sexes." [21]

[20] L. C. Pogrebin, "Rap groups," *Ms.* (March, 1973), 81.

[21] W. Farrell, "Men: Guidelines for Consciousness Raising," *Ms.* (February, 1973), 117. For a collection of articles on the problem of men and the masculine role, see J. Pleck and J. Sawyer, eds., *Men and Masculinity* (Englewood Cliffs, N.J.: Prentice-Hall, 1974).

Enriching Marriages

Current dating habits represent a prototype of the sorts of relationships we ideally expect to continue in marriage. Dating is fun, and you expect your dating partner to be one of your best friends, the two of you go to the movies, share problems, talk about your feelings, and generally spend a lot of time together.

Continuing the dating pattern, the spouse becomes (at least in the middle class) your best friend. Because occupational mobility may sever family and other ties, couples depend even more on each other: they view the marital relationship as a guarantee against loneliness and isolation. Indeed, companionship is one of the most sought-after qualities in a marital relationship.

But being married provides no guarantee against isolation. In fact, many unsuccessful marriages fail because the couple cannot or will not share feelings with each other. As one disgruntled husband said after being married for several years, "My wife Jean and I have two children, and it seems that she spends almost all her time taking care of them and the house. I also have had more responsibility at the office, and I just don't have enough time to spend with Jean and the kids the way I would like."

Additional responsibilities, including children, job, and other commitments, are interpositions between husband and wife. The spouses' responsibilities, personalities, and interests change, and this may produce unforeseen changes in the marriage. The couple inevitably has less time to spend together, and the relationship suffers. The appearance of children, for instance, represents a doubtful blessing. The wife typically devotes the major proportion of her time and energy to rearing the children. The husband, on the other hand, is not expected to participate as fully in this activity. The husband is then relegated to the role of breadwinner and occasional disciplinarian. It is not surprising that marital satisfaction improves when children are "launched" in the couple's middle years, for then the husband and wife have more time for each other.[22]

[22] B. C. Rollins and K. L. Cannon, "Marital Satisfaction over the Family Life Cycle: A Reevaluation," *Journal of Marriage and the Family*, 36 (1974), 271–82.

A number of short courses have recently been developed to promote effective communication between husbands and wives and between other intimate individuals. The goal is to promote "marriage enrichment," and individuals are encouraged to be more honest and aware of their feelings toward each other. By being encouraged to disclose to and communicate openly with each other, the partners are asked to assume more responsibility and control over the direction of their relationship. Counselors teach communication skills that the couples can use to cope with their problems. Marriage counselors are shifting their role from therapist to communication consultant. Two distinguished marriage counselors have described this new thrust:

> He [the counselor] is less and less willing to "take over" and let the couple become dependent on him. He sees the problem as squarely theirs, and they alone can solve it. They have to decide what they want in their marriage that isn't there. And they have to want it enough to work hard, both of them, to get it.[23]

Besides the deeply disturbed couple who need therapy for their marital and family problems, marriage counselors are beginning to see a new kind of couple: two partners who seek help in enhancing and deepening their relationship. A couple might say, "Our marriage isn't breaking up. We are quite sure we want to stay married. But we have both decided that we want our next 10 years together to be a whole lot better than our first 10 years have been."[24]

The Minnesota Couples Communication Program (MCCP) is a course designed to teach couples how to communicate effectively. The course was constructed by Sherod Miller, Elam Nunnally, and Daniel Wackman at the University of Minnesota. Individuals are taught to assume full responsibility for their own disclosures and to listen carefully and more accurately to what their partners have to say.[25] Couples are taught a communications system that involves

[23] D. Mace and V. Mace, *We Can Have Better Marriages if We Really Want Them* (Nashville, Tenn.: Abingdon, 1974), p. 121.

[24] *Ibid.,* p. 122.

[25] Our account of the MCCP is based mainly on instructor's and training manuals prepared and published by S. Miller, E. W. Nunnally, and D. B. Wackman (Bloomington, Minn.: Marital Resource Center, 1971, 1972).

four major levels of self-disclosure. These levels are identified by the amount of information disclosed and the predictability of the response that is expected.

The statement, "Mother came over today. She and Dad are planning to take a European vacation this year," is an example of a *conventional* communication. The statement represents a simple description and is quite superficial. The aim is to be pleasant and to make small talk.

Manipulative communication is coercive and persuasive. There is no effort to explore feelings; rather, an attempt is made to control and dominate the relationship. Understanding in the communication process is not the goal; the intent is to make oneself heard. Thus, in response to the conventional statement above, the husband could say, "What are you trying to tell me, that I can't afford to take *you* to Europe? You know we can't afford it and you are always putting me against your folks. Why do you do that?" The husband's mood when he made the manipulative statement was quite irritating. The likelihood of a quarrel developing at this moment is excellent. The wife might retort, "You know, that was a pretty stupid thing for you to say. You're wrong again." Here the response includes name calling and criticism. The person tries to protect himself while hurling epithets at the other person, or perhaps even at himself: "Yes, that was a rotten thing for me to do. I am bad."

In conventional and manipulative statements, there is no effort to identify underlying problems or to share feelings. *Speculative* and *open* statements, on the other hand, indicate a willingness to explore one's feelings and intentions and their effects on the relationship. An example of a wife using a speculative statement is, "I'm sorry that I upset you by committing us to visit my parents next weekend without asking you. I'll try not to do that again." The husband might respond, "Well, I guess I was feeling tired. Perhaps, though, we should spend more time together."

In speculative communication a problem is acknowledged, though the exploration tends to be limited. A detailed analysis of the difficulties does not occur. Open communications, though, are intended to express personal feelings. There is an honest exploration of one's own feelings as well as an effort to evoke self-disclosure by the partner. "I" statements predominate—"I feel," "I think," "I believe," "I am afraid," and so on. Here is an example of open communication between husband and wife.

WIFE: You know, Bill, I get really frightened when we argue this way. I want our marriage to work but I think that I still compare us with my parents. I can understand why you get annoyed at me for doing that. Tell me, did you get angry just over this vacation matter, or does it happen at other times? Please tell me what you feel.

HUSBAND: I feel really uptight when we have these arguments. I feel threatened when I think of your family's wealth and education. I feel ashamed when I get you upset. I really don't mean to put you down, but it seems to work out that way.

In open communication, the partners take risks by making very personal statements. They let down their defenses as they invite the other person to work with them in solving mutual difficulties.

Miller and his colleagues recently studied the effects of the MCCP on increasing couples' communication skills.[26] They wanted to know two things. First, did the course increase "recall accuracy" (sensitivity about what is communicated in conversations)? That is, will couples recognize who engaged in which of such behaviors as "expressing feelings," "yielding," and "making suggestions"? Second, did the course increase the time couples spent in "work pattern communication" (that is, speculative or open disclosures) in reconciling disagreements?

There were two different groups in the study. In the experimental group, nineteen couples were divided into four different training groups, each with its own instructor. A control group, composed of seventeen couples, did not participate in the training. The couples in the study were chosen from volunteers who had attended a premarriage lecture program at a Minneapolis hospital.

Comparisons indicated that the experimental couples increased the accuracy of their recall of what happened during their conversations more than the control couples. Couples' observational

[26] E. W. Nunnally, "Effects of Communication Training upon Interaction Awareness and Empathic Accuracy of Engaged Couples: A Field Experiment" (doctoral dissertation, University of Minnesota, 1971); and S. L. Miller, "The Effects of Communication Training in Small Groups upon Self-Disclosure and Openness in Engaged Couples' Systems of Interaction: A Field Experiment" (doctoral dissertation, University of Minnesota, 1971).

skills and sensitivity increased after taking the training program. As to work pattern communication, the experimental group's willingness to share feelings increased, but the control group's scores decreased during the same period. Participation in the training program increased a couple's willingness to explore their disagreements in an honest and open way.

These findings are particularly meaningful because they cannot be attributed to the unique skills, charisma, or other special characteristics of a single course instructor. Four different instructors were employed to train couples in the experimental condition. The major advantage of the MCCP is that it teaches couples how to improve their communication skills. The couples learn to monitor their own and their partner's feelings. They also learn a conceptual framework for understanding communication patterns in their social relationships. Couples learn a realistic system for talking and relating to each other in a more conflict-free manner.

A word of caution, though: marriage enrichment "courses" are not a panacea for marital problems; they can't guarantee marital success. Couples may learn a great deal about each other's beliefs and attitudes—and then discover that their interests are incompatible. One couple who participated in a "marriage enrichment" group reported that they felt their differences were irreconcilable after attending a number of these meetings. The husband was primarily interested in his career, and he did not want to devote the additional time to his family upon which his wife insisted. Their disagreement about life styles was fundamental, and they separated.

TRUST AND THE OPEN-MARRIAGE CONTRACT

A young college professor, married for four years, told us:

> There are some things that are better left unsaid to my wife. For instance, she and I were already married when I was going to graduate school. I met this girl in one of my classes who I got to know very well. It never came down to going to bed together, but we had lunch a few times a week and we worked together on some homework assignments. I don't think that I can ever tell my wife how close I felt to this other girl. She couldn't accept the fact that I might be interested in someone else. She'd be too jealous.

This remark illustrates the rigid expectations that spouses frequently impose on each other. Husbands and wives are supposed to be interested in each other—exclusively—and they should *never* go out alone with members of the opposite sex. They are also expected to share all their activities and relationships with each other. Nena and George O'Neill's book, *Open Marriage*,[27] includes numerous examples of traditional arrangements in which spouses make "promises only angels could keep." Unfortunately, these unrealistic expectations breed dishonesty. Each spouse eventually falls below the mark set by the partner, but maintains the semblance of meeting the partner's expectations. In contrast, the O'Neills' concept of an "open marriage" invites spouses to explore a relationship in which each individual can grow from experiences inside and outside the marriage. The spouses should be free to pursue interests, activities, and relationships even if the other is not interested. The goal is to eliminate the restrictions that couples often consider critical to maintain their marriages.

An open marriage isn't possible unless trust is built into the relationship. Trust, in turn, derives from a willingness to disclose feelings and opinions and to listen. The spouses must be honest about the kind of life that they want to make with each other. Problems will eventually emerge as the relationship evolves over time. A husband might decide to change his job in mid-career, or his wife might want him to take over the child rearing. If couples are to adjust and to retain the rewarding aspects of their intimate relationship, they must often confront new and potentially disturbing facts about themselves. The O'Neills summarize the significance of self-disclosure in improving a marriage in this statement:

> . . . you must be willing to take a new fact about your mate, even if it be a violation of your expectations concerning him, and use it as the basis for a dialogue that can lead to a more realistic and open appraisal of your relationship as people. With such a dialogue, couples can seek a better understanding of one another, one that allows them to reintegrate on a new, more open level of knowledge

[27] N. O'Neill and G. O'Neill, *Open Marriage: A New Life Style for Couples* (New York: M. Evans, 1972).

concerning one another, a level more closely approximating the full honesty that should exist between marital partners.[28]

The O'Neills presuppose that successful marriages maintain an open dialogue between partners. This approach may not work for all couples. It is possible to imagine circumstances (which have been illustrated in this chapter) when discretion should be used. If the timing of the disclosure is inappropriate, or if the disclosure will impose an unnecessary burden on the spouse, sharing intimacy may be unwise. In the long run, though, a successful intimate relationship depends on couples' being honest and open in their feelings.

[28] *Ibid.,* p. 236.

six

psychotherapy: "the talking cure"

> Optimal therapy has meant an exploration of
> increasingly strange and unknown and dangerous
> feelings. . . . [The client] becomes acquainted with
> elements of his experiences which have in the past been
> denied to awareness as too threatening, too damaging to
> the structure of the self.
>
> —Carl Rogers

Mary Ann is twenty-three and has been visiting a psychiatrist for one year. Her husband was placed in the mental ward of a local hospital after he tried to commit suicide. She was pregnant and did not want the child, so she had an abortion. She told us in an interview:

> Psychotherapy was different from any other experience in my life. I felt that the hourly sessions were my own and anything I said was important. I could talk about my feelings concerning my husband and the abortion, and it was okay to do that. I think I have a little better grasp on what happens to me. At least my problems don't weigh me down as they did before.

A businessman told us what happened when he went to a clinical psychologist:

> I kept having these blinding headaches but my doctor couldn't find anything wrong. When I talked to the therapist it came out that they occurred after some sort of conflict—an argument with my wife, or my son, or at work.

92

Another former client in psychotherapy described to us how he occasionally lied when he felt ashamed of what he had felt or done:

> There were a few times when I didn't tell him the truth because I was so ashamed. I just didn't want him to know about it. Afterwards I would go home and say, "Why the hell did I lie? Here I am paying this guy all this money." I knew if I lied that it wouldn't help, so I resolved to tell the truth the next time I went. But I didn't.

Self-disclosure is critical in helping individuals deal with severe emotional problems. Some people who have difficulties at work or at home often can't adjust to the pressures imposed on them. These people need to talk with someone about their problems. Most of the time, they approach a friend or an acquaintance for advice or support. Occasionally, because friends aren't available or because their problem is too severe, they seek help from a psychotherapist. In this chapter we will describe what happens in psychotherapy as the therapist encourages the client to explore, to understand, and, hopefully, to deal with his own problems.

SELF-DECEPTION AND EMOTIONAL PROBLEMS [1]

Most psychotherapists feel that self-disclosure is a necessary condition of progress in therapy. The therapist, by his warmth, acceptance, understanding, and occasional interpretation, will help the client look at and discover himself. For example, the individual may learn that negative feelings toward certain relatives are due to demands that they made on him in the past. With this realization, he can deal with the guilt and shame that these feelings cause in him. As he develops self-confidence and a new outlook on himself, his behavior, thoughts, and feelings toward others become less defensive.

A major cause of emotional problems is concealment. We dislike some things about our personalities—how we look, how we feel, or

---

[1] In writing this section, the authors found the ideas of Carl Rogers and William H. Fitts on the process of psychotherapy extremely useful. See C. R. Rogers, "A Process Conception of Psychotherapy," *American Psychologist,* 13 (1958), 142–49; and W. H. Fitts, *The Experience of Psychotherapy* (Princeton, N.J.: Van Nostrand, 1965).

how we behave. We hide these "flaws" because we are afraid that important people in our lives—friends, family, co-workers, classmates, or acquaintances—will reject us. Instead, we wear masks and play roles, such as "good son," "loving wife," "successful businessman," or "loyal friend," in order to earn the approval of others.

Unfortunately, we frequently succeed in deceiving ourselves when we play these roles. We hide information about ourselves that might produce anxiety, frighten us, or lead to rejection by others. These negative feelings, experiences, and emotions do not lie hidden quietly. They continue to affect our behavior in ways that we cannot control: dizzy spells, feelings of uneasiness, tension—all represent the expression of impulses that we try to deny. Years of concealment eventually take their toll. A person may feel exhausted, confused, uncertain about his future, angry at his friends. At this point, some individuals may even consider suicide. Many, seeking relief desperately, turn to a psychotherapist.

Frequently, clients have ambivalent feelings about therapy. They approach the therapist with some specific problem—for instance, a problem with sex, family, or work. The client may prefer to talk superficially about his general background, other people, or physical symptoms, because he can talk about these topics without feeling threatened. Yet as clients participate in therapy, they often find that these issues are secondary. The real problems are more fundamental and less easy to discuss.

Clients are often ashamed and embarrassed about their feelings. They may have learned that feeling angry, hostile, jealous, or weak is inappropriate and "bad." The awareness, "I don't like my parents," or, "I am afraid," is threatening because it doesn't fit the individual's self-concept. To admit these thoughts can be terrifying. Individuals may think, "I can't say these things. The therapist is going to think that I am a terrible person." Or they may ask themselves, "Can I accept the criticism and pain of finding out what I am really like?" A former client of Carl Rogers gave this account of the mixture of anticipation and dread one feels when disclosing highly sensitive information:

> I remember a good deal of emotional tension in the second interview, where I first mentioned homosexuality. I remember that I felt drawn

down into myself, into places I didn't want to go, hadn't quite been to before, and yet had to see. I think I dreaded this interview because I had been so afraid before counseling began that I would get to that subject. And afraid that I wouldn't.[2]

Virtually all therapists, regardless of their approach or theoretical orientation, agree that the creation of rapport is essential for the client to explore suppressed feelings. The client must trust the therapist and respect him. In addition, he must feel that the therapist respects him. For his part, the therapist should feel comfortable with the client and should be able to accept his self-disclosures objectively and nonjudgmentally.

Before disclosing intimate information about themselves, clients may test the therapist to determine whether or not he can be trusted. Even in the first session, clients may describe what "horrible persons" they are in order to shock the therapist. Overcoming this obstacle may be a major determinant in the formation of a successful relationship between therapist and client. A therapist reported to us her reactions to this testing period.

> Clients will come in and tell you some wild things they have done. A man will say, "I really do beat my wife," or a woman will say, "I have had I don't know how many affairs." They expect you to go, "Ugh—heavenly days, you *are* an awful person." And you kinda just sit there and say, "Um-huh," or, "Oh, really." You don't flare up or say, "I can't stand you; get out of here." What I do is ask them how they feel about their statements. I don't condemn them.

Clients who fear the consequences of intimate disclosure may attempt to sabotage the therapy process by avoiding critical self-disclosures until the last few minutes of a session.[3] This gives the client control over the relationship. He can mention what bothers him, but he does not have to pursue these feelings in any depth. In a sense, the defensive client says, "Look, everything that has gone on before is not what I wanted to talk about. Now I am going to lay this on you really fast and then I am going to get up and leave."

---

[2] C. R. Rogers, *Client-Centered Therapy* (Boston: Houghton Mifflin, 1951), p. 72.

[3] K. N. Anchor and H. M. Sandler, "Psychotherapy Sabotage and Avoidance of Self-Disclosure," *Proceedings,* 81st Annual Convention of the American Psychological Association, 1973, pp. 483–84.

Withholding information until the closing minutes can also be a test, as if the client were saying, "If you (the therapist) really care for me, you will extend my time." Therapists whom we interviewed reported to us that they confront such clients with this problem, asking them why they are doing this or asking them to begin talking about the topic in question at the beginning of the next session. One therapist told us:

> What I want to tell the client is, "I recognize that things are hard for you to talk about and I would rather you speak more about them when we have more time to work on them and work them through." This also says to him, "I know you haven't fully reached talking readiness early in the hour and I hope that you will look at this as part of your defenses and that this is something we can work on together."

As a client discovers that the therapy session provides a supportive atmosphere for talking openly, he may unexpectedly acknowledge previously hidden information about himself and his feelings toward others. Clients may say, "I never thought of talking about these things before." As the client talks freely about sensitive matters, the intensity of the experience may cause physical agitation such as crying, trembling, or sweating.

The individual who explores intimate areas learns that he is not despicable and that expressing his feelings will not lead to rejection by the therapist. The client's concept of himself changes as he becomes aware of and accepts feelings that have previously been too threatening.

Many former clients mentioned to us that verbalizing their feelings helped. A woman who survived a nearly fatal illness in childhood explained to us how she dealt with her feelings toward a sister who died at the age of fourteen:

> My sister had been chronically ill her whole life, and she died when I was twenty. Afterwards, I found it very hard to think about her without feeling really depressed. In therapy I explored this, even though it was painful. I came to realize that a lot of my depression was caused by guilt—guilt because I was healthy and she wasn't, and because we used to fight a lot. Getting it out like that helped me to understand why I reacted the way I did and also helped me to see that my guilt was really unjustified.

I remember leaving the therapy session feeling greatly relieved. For the first time, I could think about my sister without being depressed. I could think about her life and the good things about it without feeling guilty.

An important value of therapy is that it expands the individual's willingness to talk about himself. In a type of extinction or "unlearning" process, the individual learns to express feelings in a nonpunitive atmosphere. In the past, the client may have feared rejection or criticism and thus suppressed his feelings. But in the presence of a warm, supportive, and friendly therapist, he can express his feelings without fearing disapproval. Thus, the threatening quality of self-disclosure is reduced in therapy.

Ideally, if the client's therapy is successful, he spends more time talking about his positive qualities. The client no longer dwells on the reactions of others as a guide for his actions. His talk reflects increased self-confidence and autonomy: he refers to his own decisions and plans for the future. He may discuss ideas for a new job, improving relations with friends and family, and other positive changes. Psychologically, he replaces negative self-references ("I am bad," "This feeling is terrible") with positive ones ("I am okay," "I can understand and accept why I feel this way"). The momentum started in therapy will hopefully transfer to day-to-day living as the client's need for professional assistance decreases.

SELF-DISCLOSURE AND THERAPY OUTCOME

Most forms of psychotherapy assume that emotional problems can be reduced by encouraging increased self-disclosure by the patient. The role of the therapist is to facilitate the patient's willingness to explore and understand his feelings and actions. This technique is the basis of "the talking cure" pioneered by Sigmund Freud, the founder of psychoanalysis. More recently, psychotherapists such as Carl Rogers, Sidney Jourard, and O. H. Mowrer have advocated the value of openness in successful psychotherapy.

A number of studies[4] confirm the relationship between level of

[4] See C. B. Truax and R. R. Carkhuff, *Toward Effective Counseling and Psychotherapy* (Chicago: Aldine, 1967), for a review of the pertinent literature.

self-disclosure in psychotherapy and constructive personality change. This research is necessarily correlational. A study by Charles Truax and Robert Carkhuff [5] illustrates typical research in this area. Ratings of self-disclosure were obtained from a series of psychotherapy sessions between patients at a mental hospital and different therapists. The patients in the study were diagnosed as schizophrenics, who are characterized by withdrawal, distorted thought processes, and the breakdown of integrated personality functioning. The level of self-disclosure by patients in these therapy sessions was rated by judges who heard tape recordings of the sessions and then applied the Truax Depth of Intrapersonal Exploration Scale (DX). In their study, Truax and Carkhuff give some examples of low, medium, and high levels of patient self-disclosure, according to the DX scale:

Low. The patient actively evades personally relevant material (. . . by changing the subject, refusing to respond at all, etc.). . . . The patient does not respond to personally relevant material even when the therapist speaks of it.

Medium. Personally relevant material is discussed (volunteered in part or in whole). . . . Both the emotional remoteness and the mechanical manner of the patient makes his discussion often sound rehearsed.

High. The patient is . . . actively exploring his feelings, his values, his perceptions of others, his relationships, his fears, his turmoil, and his life choices.

Patients who were rated high in self-disclosure showed greater constructive personality change across a variety of recovery measures, including the Rorschach projective test, the MMPI (Minnesota Multiphasic Personality Inventory), and the percentage of time hospitalized. Another potentially important finding occurred: as early as the second psychotherapy session, a patient's likelihood of recovering could be predicted by his level of self-disclosure. It may be that high levels of self-disclosure in early stages of therapy are a sign of a patient's readiness to improve.

Though research indicates that self-exploration should be gener-

[5] C. B. Truax and R. R. Carkhuff, "Client and Therapist Transparency in the Psychotherapeutic Encounter," *Journal of Counseling Psychology,* 12 (1965), 3–9.

ally encouraged in therapy, the therapist must ultimately decide whether a particular patient has the strength to look at himself. Some individuals may need to keep secrets hidden in order to maintain an acceptable level of personality functioning. The therapist must therefore be fully aware of why he wants certain material to be brought out and why the client has set up defenses. If the therapist is convinced that it is necessary to dismantle the client's defenses, he should possess the skill to help the client cope with his hidden feelings, no matter how painful they are. The process of rebuilding a shattered personality is usually more difficult than the shattering process itself: as one therapist told us, "Sure, it is great sport to let people bring everything out, but if you and they don't know what to do with it, it can be very dangerous."

CONTRASTING VIEWS ON SELF-DISCLOSURE IN THERAPY

Modern approaches to psychotherapy differ on a number of issues: therapeutic goals, who should be accepted for treatment, the relationship between therapist and client, and what to talk about in therapy. In this section we will examine the contrasting views of two major approaches to psychotherapy—psychoanalysis and client-centered therapy—on the role of self-disclosure.

Freud's approach[6] to therapy was based on the notion that unconscious processes were largely responsible for one's behavior. To a large extent, the aim of psychoanalysis was to make the unconscious conscious so that an individual could deal with his feelings and control them. Freud asked his patients to follow the fundamental rule of free association: the patient allows his thoughts to flow freely, reporting honestly whatever comes to mind. Freud felt that all thoughts and feelings were connected in some way; even "irrelevant" or "frivolous" material fitted into a central theme. Ultimately, the patient's verbalizations could be used to trace the source of his problems, typically some early childhood experiences.

Imagine that you decide to enter psychoanalysis. Here is how an analyst might instruct you to free associate:

[6] An excellent introduction to Freud's psychoanalytic theory is D. H. Ford and H. V. Urban, *Systems of Psychotherapy: A Comparative Study* (New York: John Wiley, 1963).

In ordinary conversations, you usually try to keep a connecting thread running through your remarks, excluding any intrusive ideas or side issues, so as not to wander too far from the point, and rightly so. But in this case you must talk differently. As you talk, various thoughts will occur to you which you would like to ignore because of certain criticisms and objections. You will be tempted to think, "that is irrelevant, or unimportant, or nonsensical," and to avoid saying it. Do not give in to such criticisms. Report such thoughts in spite of your wish not to do so. Later, the reason for this injunction, the only one you have to follow, will become clear. Report whatever goes through your mind. Pretend you are a traveler, describing to someone beside you the changing views which you see outside the train window. Never forget your promise "to be absolutely honest, and never leave anything out" because it seems unpleasant to talk about.[7]

Early in his career, Freud noted that in spite of the therapist's admonitions about being honest, patients hid information about themselves. Patients might use long pauses, switch topics abruptly, or avoid completely certain sensitive material. Along with this resistance, a phenomenon known as "transference" would occur. The patient would avoid discussing his conflicts by acting them out. The patient would relive events associated with important persons in his life, with the analyst symbolizing each such person. For instance, female patients might express affection and a desire for sexual intercourse with the therapist. A fifty-one-year-old widow who carried on a flirtation with her therapist reported to us, "It was really kind of a funny relationship. I would tell him things, almost as if he were my former husband. I would apologize about why I couldn't have sex. I wanted him to tell me that I wasn't a bad wife, and that I was important in his life." After her husband's death, this woman had had a number of casual affairs. She was acting out in therapy how she related to other men and to her husband.

The therapist who has control of the situation can use the transference relationship to gain insight into the patient's problems. Indeed, Freud saw transference as an important part of the therapeutic process. In order to facilitate transference and the patient's free associations, the therapist was supposed to avoid any

[7] *Ibid.,* p. 168.

self-disclosure. The therapist was to sit behind the patient, avoid eye contact, and *never* reveal personal information about himself. The therapist should "be impenetrable to the patient, and, like a mirror, reflect nothing but what is shown to him." [8] This approach protected the therapist from becoming emotionally involved or even embarrassed by the patient's disclosures. Its main purpose, however, was to encourage the patient's fantasies and to foster the transference relationship.

Freud did not want the therapist's behavior to influence the patient's disclosure; therefore, he viewed the therapist as an aloof figure, neutral and impersonal in his reactions, as well as nontalkative. He should "take as a model in psycho-analytic treatment the surgeon who puts aside all his feelings, including that of human sympathy, and concentrates his mind on one single purpose, that of performing the operation as skillfully as possible." [9]

In contrast with psychoanalysis, client-centered therapy emphasizes therapist honesty in relating to clients. The therapist should not hide behind a professional façade to avoid sharing feelings with the client. The therapist's role is to demonstrate that he cares. He helps the client discover and understand for himself the emotions he feels. The client's problem is based in his need to conceal and to deceive others and himself about his true feelings. The therapist who is a model of integrated and nondefensive behavior can provide a valuable example for the patient to change his own behavior.

The client-centered approach based on the work of Carl Rogers advocates a close interpersonal relationship between therapist and client.[10] The therapist's role is not to probe, analyze, or interpret, but to listen supportively as a person explores the sources and solutions to his problems. The term "client," as opposed to "patient," emphasizes the respect and capacity for self-direction attributed to the individual. The therapist who communicates

---

[8] S. Freud, "Recommendations for Physicians on the Psycho-Analytic Method of Treatment," in *Collected Papers*, Vol. 2 (London: Hogarth Press, 1956), p. 331.

[9] *Ibid.*, p. 327.

[10] Two useful introductions to client-centered therapy are C. R. Rogers, *Client-Centered Therapy* (Boston: Houghton Mifflin, 1951); and C. R. Rogers, *On Becoming a Person* (Boston: Houghton Mifflin, 1961).

respect and support will reduce the client's defensiveness and provide a nonthreatening context within which he can understand and accept himself. The therapist must show that he cares about and understands the client's problems. He must also be "genuine": he must divulge personal feelings that affect his relationship with the client. Rogers and Truax have emphasized this need to be genuine. .

> . . . so if I sense that I am feeling bored by my contacts with this client and this feeling persists, I think I owe it to him and to our relationship to share this feeling with him. The same would hold if my feeling is one of being afraid of this client, or if my attention is so focused on my own problems that I can scarcely listen to him. But as I attempt to share these feelings I also want to be constantly in touch with what is going on in me. If I am I will recognize that it is my feeling of being bored which I am expressing, and not some supposed fact about him as a boring person. If I voice it as my own reaction, it has the potentiality of leading to a deep relationship. But this feeling exists in the context of a complex and changing flow, and this needs to be communicated, too. I would like to share with him my distress at feeling bored and the discomfort I feel in expressing this aspect of me. As I share these attitudes I find that my feeling of boredom arises from my sense of remoteness from him and that I would like to be more in touch with him and even as I try to express these feelings they change. I am certainly not bored as I wait with eagerness and perhaps a bit of apprehension for his response. I also feel a new sensitivity to him now that I have shared this feeling which has been a barrier between us. I am very much more able to hear the surprise or perhaps the hurt in his voice as he now finds himself speaking more genuinely because I have dared to be real to him. I have let myself be a person—real, imperfect—in my relationship with him.[11]

Rogers and his followers consider the personal characteristics of the therapist (including warmth, empathy, and genuineness) to be more important to client self-disclosure and treatment outcome

---

[11] C. R. Rogers and C. B. Truax, "The Therapeutic Conditions Antecedent to Change: A Theoretic View," in C. R. Rogers et al., eds., *The Therapeutic Relationship and Its Impact: A Study of Psychotherapy with Schizophrenics* (Madison, Wisc.: University of Wisconsin Press, 1967).

than the therapist's professional training (for instance, in psychoanalysis or client-centered therapy). A wide range of studies support the view that the therapist's attitude and behavior toward the client are critical.[12]

An experimental study by Truax and Carkhuff [13] demonstrates how therapist warmth and empathy increase a client's willingness to talk about problems. Three different psychiatric patients (a psychotic and two patients who were severely depressed) were seen for a one-hour psychotherapeutic interview. The patient's baseline levels of self-disclosure were established during the first twenty minutes, when the therapist was warm and understanding. Therapist warmth and empathy were lowered for the next twenty-minute period. Finally, the normally high levels of therapist warmth and empathy were reintroduced in the final twenty minutes. Judges— who did not know which time period the tape recordings came from—used the Truax DX scale to rate the intimacy of the patient's statements. As predicted, all three patients decreased their self-disclosure in the second time period. But when high levels of therapist warmth and empathy were reintroduced in the final twenty minutes of the interview, the clients again became more open.

Our interviews with persons who had been in therapy tend to substantiate these results. The warm and supportive therapist fosters an atmosphere in which the client can work out his problems; cold and aloof therapists inhibit disclosure. As one client told us:

> I think another therapist could have brought me out more to face my problems. Somebody who was less objective, less disinterested. I felt as if he were timing himself when he was with me. I felt that he liked me, but I didn't have that feeling that I have with a human being with whom I can relate. And I want to relate to someone if I am going to tell him my innermost thoughts. I don't think that I really communicated with him. He was so detached.

[12] See Truax and Carkhuff, *Toward Effective Counseling and Psychotherapy;* and, for an updated review, C. B. Truax and K. M. Mitchell, "Research on Certain Therapist Interpersonal Skills in Relation to Process and Outcome," in A. E. Bergin and S. L. Garfield, eds., *Handbook of Psychotherapy and Behavior Change: An Empirical Analysis* (New York: John Wiley, 1971).

[13] C. B. Truax and R. C. Carkhuff, "Experimental Manipulation of Therapeutic Conditions," *Journal of Counseling Psychology,* 29 (1965), 119–24.

In contrast, a young man told us that the therapist's warmth helped him to explore his feelings.

> Right from the start, I felt that she really cared about me. She seemed to be upset by my problems and to be happy when I made progress. I felt so relaxed with her that it was easy to talk about very personal things.

In addition to the therapist's warmth and empathy, his genuineness or nondefensiveness in the relationship influences client self-disclosure. Therapists who don't act phony minimize the threatening aspects of the encounter for the client.

"Therapist genuineness" describes how much of what the therapist says agrees with what he is feeling. On a five-point scale that measures this characteristic, a "phony" therapist "is clearly defensive in the interaction and there is explicit evidence of a very considerable discrepancy between his experiencing and his current verbalizations. Thus, the therapist makes striking contradictions in statements . . . ." In contrast, the "genuine therapist is *freely and deeply himself* in the relationship. There is an openness to *experiences and feelings* by the therapist of all types—without traces of defensiveness or retreat into professionalism." [14]

To examine the relationship between therapist genuineness and the depth of self-disclosure by patients, Truax and Carkhuff [15] examined a sample of 306 therapy sessions involving sixteen hospitalized psychiatric patients. The correlations between the average level of therapist genuineness and the average level of patient self-disclosure was moderately strong (r = .43). The nondefensive therapist was able to evoke a greater depth of self-disclosure from the patient in a therapy session.

The results of the studies on client-centered therapy emphasize the valuable role of an intimate therapist-client relationship. The client needs to know that the therapist cares, and that the therapist is not playing a game of one-upmanship. The therapist who is silent and "professionally neutral" doesn't communicate that he cares very effectively. Patients may ask, and be unable to answer, these

[14] Truax and Carkhuff, "Client and Therapist Transparency in the Psychotherapeutic Encounter," p. 7.
[15] *Ibid.*

questions if the therapist doesn't show his concern: "Does he really understand my problems?" "Does he respect me enough to say what he feels about me?" "Does he like me or hate me for what I have been saying?" "Should I disclose my feelings?"

THERAPIST SELF-DISCLOSURE

The genuine therapist is authentic and honest in dealing with the client. He doesn't suppress or withhold feelings that are relevant to the therapeutic session. However, the genuine therapist does not necessarily divulge personal information about his own life history, family relationships, or problems.

Some therapists feel that therapist self-disclosure is a valuable technique in facilitating client self-exploration. This procedure is an example of the well-established phenomenon of disclosure reciprocity (see Chapter Three). It may be easier for the client to explore and accept certain experiences if the therapist can disclose to the client that he struggled with the same or similar problems in the past. Arthur Burton has illustrated how this process works:

CLIENT: My mother is a bitch. Because she couldn't love my old man she put me in his place. And I tried to fill it. Now look at me today: neither man nor woman.

THERAPIST: Your mother needed somebody and found you.

CLIENT: Did you know that I slept in the same bed with her until I was eight years old. Wow!

THERAPIST: (Silence)

CLIENT: I'm fine, and then she phones and I'm right back where I started. She can undo six months of work in two seconds.

THERAPIST: My mother was a problem, too.

CLIENT: Your mother!

THERAPIST: Yep. She didn't find intimacy with my father and looked to me for things he couldn't give her. Oedipus had a rough time in my family.

CLIENT: Then you know what I'm talking about.

THERAPIST: From personal experience.[16]

To illustrate further, a therapist told us about an adolescent boy

[16] A. Burton, *Interpersonal Psychotherapy* (Englewood Cliffs, N.J.: Prentice-Hall, 1972), pp. 100–101.

who had described to him various fantasies he had about murdering other persons, including his mother. The therapist reacted this way:

> I disclosed a very frightening experience which I had when I was in my teens. I had what seemed to be an irresistible impulse to kill somebody, which, needless to say, I didn't do. That was really a turning point. He asked me how I controlled my murderous impulses. From then on, it became much more of a trusting relationship.

In this case, the therapist's disclosure accomplished two purposes. First, the rapport between client and therapist was strengthened, and, second, the boy learned that his fantasies were not unique, that even a respectable and admired adult once had similar thoughts. In spite of the advantages, there are some drawbacks to self-disclosure by psychotherapists. Freudian psychoanalysts fear, for instance, that the therapist might react to the patient on the basis of his own problems—a phenomenon known as "countertransference." A primary Freudian concern was that the patient's self-disclosures should stem from his own life experience. The therapist, according to psychoanalysis, should display a neutral and impersonal attitude in order to encourage such spontaneous verbalizations.

Another difficulty with therapist self-disclosure is reflected in the view that the therapist should never burden the patient with his problems; the client should not leave the session absorbed with problems other than his own. Therapist disclosure of personal problems might, as one psychoanalyst noted, "degenerate into a mutual analysis because this makes heavy emotional demands on the patient, and with some types of patients . . . the analysis could easily become . . . an analysis of the analyst." [17]

Given the variety of patients that therapists see, it is impossible to make a blanket statement about the effectiveness of therapist self-disclosure. Its usefulness depends on its timing, the specific problem of the patient, and the content of the self-disclosure.

Some recent studies indicate that the timing of therapist self-disclosure is important. Patients expect therapists to maintain

---

[17] C. Thompson, *Psychoanalysis: Evolution and Development* (New York: Grove Press, 1950), p. 187.

some "psychological distance," at least in the early stages of psychotherapy. Some clients view therapist self-disclosure as unusual and inappropriate in the beginning of therapy, particularly if client and therapist have never met each other before. The ultimate effect of therapist self-disclosure in an early session may be to inhibit self-disclosure by the wary patient.

Norman Simonson and Susan Bahr of the University of Massachusetts conducted a study[18] that tested this idea. Subjects in a study on psychotherapy processes heard a twenty-minute tape recording ostensibly containing excerpts from a first therapy session between their therapist and another person. The tapes had been prepared in advance by the therapist and an actress who played the patient. One group heard a tape in which the therapist made some nonintimate comments about his background; this constituted the "demographic disclosure" condition. A second group heard a tape recording in which the therapist revealed personal information about his background ("personal disclosure" condition). After listening to the tape recording, subjects were interviewed by the therapist. The interviews were recorded, and judges later rated the subjects' degree of disclosure. As part of the same study, subjects were asked to rate how much they liked the therapist.

Personal disclosure by the therapist produced *lower* levels of patient self-disclosure and therapist attractiveness than in the demographic disclosure condition. The reversal of disclosure reciprocity in this study (that is, high therapist disclosure lowered rather than increased patient self-disclosure tendencies) is an important finding. As Simonson and Bahr noted, "Therapist disclosure that was regarded as comfortable and 'human' in demographic disclosure became frightening or at least disquieting when the level of disclosure was increased in the personal disclosure condition. The level of therapist disclosure went too far beyond the subjects' expectations for this professional relationship—at least during an initial session." As therapy progresses, patients may have a kinder view of therapist disclosure. Patients may feel that material

[18] N. R. Simonson and S. Bahr, "Self-Disclosure by the Professional and Paraprofessional Therapist," *Journal of Consulting and Clinical Psychology*, 42 (1974), 359–63.

that was originally unacceptable to talk about may be helpful and appropriate at later stages of the relationship.

The "intimacy equilibrium" hypothesis of Michael Argyle and Janet Dean provides a useful explanation of these results.[19] This view holds that individuals maintain an optimal degree of intimacy in their relationship with others (in terms of self-disclosure, eye contact, physical distance, and so forth). If one person oversteps the limits of acceptable intimacy, then the other person will withdraw. Similarly, patients may shun disclosure if they believe that the therapist is accelerating intimacy at an unacceptable rate.

What a therapist tells the client about himself may also affect the therapist-client relationship. Imagine how you would feel if a therapist talked about this list of topics:

1. The kind of person he would like to be.
2. The things that make him especially proud of himself.
3. Whether or not he is able to let himself go when he gets angry.
4. His feelings about how much independence he needs.
5. Whether or not he ever cried as an adult when he was sad.

In contrast, how would you feel if the therapist talked about topics from this second list?

1. His feelings of prejudice toward particular members in the group.
2. His distrust of a group member.
3. Past failure experiences as a group (therapy) leader.
4. The fact that he is currently in therapy for personal problems.
5. His feelings of being inferior to other members in the group.

Research conducted by Robert Dies[20] at the University of Maryland on group psychotherapy indicates that people react more favorably to a therapist who divulges personal information based on items in the first rather than the second list. Therapist disclosure of "normal" feelings—feelings of loneliness, sadness, anger, positive

---

[19] M. Argyle and J. Dean, "Eye Contact, Distance, and Affiliation," *Sociometry,* 28 (1965), 289–304.

[20] R. R. Dies and L. Cohen, "Content Considerations in Group Therapist Self-Disclosure" (Paper presented at the 81st Annual Convention of the American Psychological Association, 1973).

strivings, and so forth—is appreciated. Statements about the therapist's inferiority, hostility, lack of emotional stability, or attacks on patients in group psychotherapy are considered inappropriate.

Other important factors in evaluating the effectiveness of therapist self-disclosure include how the therapist's disclosure fits into the context of what the patient says, and whether the patient expects the therapist to reveal himself. Research in this area has barely begun.

THERAPISTS AND THE PURCHASE OF FRIENDSHIP

Many people who have problems never seek out a mental health professional. They turn to clergymen, physicians, teachers, or friends. This may explain the apparent spontaneous recoveries of troubled persons who do not consult a psychotherapist. Their progress may be due to a nonprofessional's help and advice. In interviews with college students, we repeatedly heard how young people would talk to dormitory roommates, friends, and relatives about their personal problems. Carl Rogers argued in a significant paper that the basic variables of therapist warmth, understanding, and nondefensiveness are necessary for successful recovery.[21] Since a person may also find these qualities in very close friends, it may well be that a good friend is better equipped (and certainly more accessible and less expensive) than a trained therapist with college degrees, diplomas, and certificates!

A therapist-client relationship may fill a gap in an individual's life. Because of the mobility in our society, our relationships tend to be shallow. Many people feel very lonely and alienated and do not have very meaningful relationships. They need someone with whom they can let their hair down and not be rejected. It is possible that some people seek to buy support and friendship in the guise of psychotherapy. As one psychotherapist candidly explained to us: "It makes a good deal of sense to talk about the therapist being a bit like a prostitute. The prostitute is being paid for sexual services, the therapist is being paid for friendship services."

---

[21] C. R. Rogers, "The Necessary and Sufficient Conditions of Therapeutic Personality Change," *Journal of Consulting Psychology,* 21 (1957), 95–103.

Another therapist descibed a young boy whom he had seen in therapy. Now the boy comes into the office and just sits in the waiting room. The office has become "home" for him, a place where he flips through magazines and talks to the staff.

One of the problems in viewing therapy as a paid friendship is that a client may not want to get well. The person may want to continue to come and pay money in order to maintain the relationship. The client may say to the therapist, "You know, you are the only friend in the world I can talk to." Unfortunately, this attitude fosters an excessive reliance on the therapist and a resistance to getting well. Recovery must eventually mean independence and the breaking up of this friendship.

It seems a great shame that we cannot take greater advantage of friendships, given their potential therapeutic value. In general, people may benefit from talking to a close friend about their problems. According to a prominent psychotherapist,

> It is not dangerous for people to talk to each other about their problems. The person who shares his perplexities with one close and respected friend is more likely to be helped rather than harmed. If his needs exceed what can be afforded by the therapy the experience is more likely rather than less likely to encourage him toward expert counsel.[22]

Of course, confiding in friends involves risks, as we saw in Chapter Four. Our friends may be unable to see our problems objectively because they are so close to us. Often, our problems may be threatening to them. In general, a relationship should be both strong and stable before intimate confidences are exchanged. Psychotherapy is popular because such relationships are not ordinarily available.

PSYCHOTHERAPY: LEARNING TO EXPLORE FEELINGS

Entering psychotherapy is a big decision for an individual. He realizes that his problems are serious and that he cannot cope with

---

[22] W. Schofield, *Psychotherapy: The Purchase of Friendship* (Englewood Cliffs, N.J.: Prentice-Hall, 1964), p. 162.

them alone. He needs help. The client's expectations about the therapist, however, may be exaggerated. He may view the therapist as a powerful figure who will administer a magical cure.

But the therapist uses no tricks. He does not guarantee a cure. He does, though, offer confidentiality and support. He listens, cares, and hopes to understand the client's experiences. Therapy may represent for some clients the first meaningful relationship of this kind in their lives. They can express openly feelings that other persons may never have understood or noticed.

The time required to talk about oneself may take many sessions. The process of self-exploration may be a painful struggle. With a supportive therapist the client can begin to lower his defenses. He may discover experiences that he never recognized consciously, and these discoveries may shock him. The client will have more control of his life when he can understand himself. The following poem by therapist Louise White conveys the importance of self-disclosure and psychotherapy from the client's point of view.

The cards are down—
seven secret stacks.

This game was started long ago
before I knew you.

The gamble is a big one;
All that I am
For all that I can be.

I know the cards on top;
Those I can see and handle quickly.
But as long as cards underneath
lie unturned, unknown,
I cannot win.

Do I play
against myself
or
with myself?

Do not tell me, please,
to play the red eight
on the black nine.

Just sit with me as I hesitate,
And wait as I wait.
I cannot hurry,
For I have so much more at stake than you.[23]

[23] From W. H. Fitts, *The Experience of Psychotherapy*, pp. 55–56. © 1965; reprinted by permission of D. Van Nostrand Co.

seven

new styles of intimacy: groups and communes

Loneliness and alienation appear to be by-products of our modern, technological society. People feel estranged from one another; the average city dweller sees thousands of people every week but may feel close to none of them. Indeed, the rise in the number of people seeing psychotherapists, chronicled in Chapter Six, may be due in part to the alienating nature of urban life. To counter these conditions, many Americans have begun participating in activities designed, at least in part, to foster intimacy and closeness among people. In this chapter, we will discuss two of the most prominent innovations—experiential groups and communal living. Both have the ambitious goals of bringing people closer together, fostering a spirit of group unity and understanding, and improving the quality of life for their members. Experiential groups are less radical an activity than communal living—they do not require such a complete and utter change in life style—but the aim of achieving intimacy with others is no less of a priority. In both groups and communes, the manner in which self-disclosure is handled may determine the success or failure of the enterprise. The value of an experiential group and the life span of a commune depend in part on whether the members are open or closed with one another about their feelings.

EXPERIENTIAL GROUPS
A Shortcut to Sharing

The concept of the experiential group originated after World War II and was implemented in 1947 with the founding of the National Training Laboratory for Group Development, but the movement did not show any dramatic growth until the 1960s. Originally, the experiential group was seen as a vehicle for learning how groups function, as a method for human relations training, or as a way to increase group productivity. Over time, however, the social-psychological origins of the group movement assumed less importance; clinical psychologists and others with a mental health orientation began seeing the group experience as a way to promote personality change, to enhance individual growth, and to foster intimacy between persons.

Experiential groups go by many names: sensitivity training or "T" groups, encounter groups, human relations training, marathon groups. We are using the term "experiential group" as an umbrella to refer to the whole range of group experiences. However, it must be noted that groups differ widely. The more "conservative" ones, often called sensitivity or human relations training, are oriented toward improving interpersonal skills and understanding group processes. Encounter groups, on the other hand, stress emotional expression; often, nonverbal exercises are encouraged as a way of promoting emotional sensitivity. The goals of encounter groups usually include self-awareness and self-actualization. Though it is important to note that such differences between experiential groups do exist, our discussion will focus on the similarities between these groups, rather than the differences.

WHAT HAPPENS IN AN EXPERIENTIAL GROUP?

One way to find out what happens in groups is to ask individuals who have been in them. We interviewed many participants, and one young woman named Joan described how her group started.

> At first we all sat around making small talk and cracking jokes. Then we introduced ourselves to each other. Then, there was this long silence for almost twenty minutes, until one guy turned to the leader and got really angry with him. He said he was wasting his time and money, and that the leader should take over and "get the show on the road," I think was the way he put it.
>
> But the leader said it was *our* show, not his, and we had to do it our own way. Then, a man started to criticize the first guy, and he asked him why he had to organize things and why he was so compulsive. Then, other people started talking and we really got going!

The lack of structure that the man in Joan's group found so disturbing is a key element in most experiential groups. A group of people convene with no agenda, no rules, and no prescribed way to behave. Such an experience is unfamiliar to most of us, and usually generates much anxiety. Social comparison processes start operating. "What do they think of me?" "How should I act?" "What are they doing here?" "Are they nervous too?" These are typical questions running through one's mind when the first session starts. A lawyer described to us his feelings at the start of the group he joined.

> None of us knew what the hell to do. We all kept sneaking looks at each other to see how everyone was reacting. Finally, one guy said he felt nervous and uncomfortable. Another guy said he did too. And then we all relaxed and felt better.

Lack of structure is itself a motivating force. Feeling uncomfortable in such an ambiguous setting, the group members begin to interact, to find out what everyone else is thinking and, often, to impose some structure on the group.

A critical element separating the group experience from day-to-day interactions is the lack of norms regulating ordinary social behavior. We rarely tell a person how he makes us feel, or reveal intimate feelings, or become intensely emotional in front of strangers. If we criticize another, we often do so in the guise of faint praise or with a great deal of tact. Persons who do not conform to these rules are guilty of what one sociologist calls "social improprieties," [1] and are usually avoided as strange or unpredictable. In the extreme, such persons may be regarded as mentally ill and may be hospitalized. Yet in an experiential group, such rules do not apply, as a noted sociologist has written:

> . . . taboos of ordinary society are reversed: frankness substitutes for tact, self-expression for manners, nonverbal techniques for language, and immediacy for responsibility. Norms that have evolved to ensure the smooth and continual operation of society are rejected. [2]

Although experiential groups presumably have no norms or behavioral rules governing them, implicit norms *do* exist. The most important norm concerns self-disclosure. Members must be willing to reveal their feelings, their thoughts, and sometimes even their pasts, or possibly risk the censure of the group. Carl Rogers, one of the most respected advocates of the group movement, has explained this norm:

> As time goes on, the group finds it unbearable that any member should live behind a mask or front. The polite words, the intellectual understanding of each other and of relationships, the smooth coin of tact and cover-up—amply satisfactory for interactions outside—are just not good enough. . . . Gently at times, almost savagely at others, the group *demands* that the individual be himself, that his current feelings not be hidden, that he remove the mask of ordinary social intercourse. [3]

Another norm prevalent in most (but not all) groups is an emphasis on emotional expression, often at the expense of cognitive expression. Intellectualizing one's reactions ("head games") is not accepted. One is expected to express his feelings, even negative ones, about himself or others in the group.

The group fosters a permissive atmosphere in which participants are free to express their feelings, try out new behaviors, ask questions, and discover themselves. Ideally, the usual threat associ-

---

[1] E. Goffman, *Interaction Ritual* (Chicago: Aldine, 1967).

[2] K. W. Back, *Beyond Words* (Baltimore: Penguin, 1972), p. 31.

[3] C. R. Rogers, *Carl Rogers on Encounter Groups* (New York: Harper & Row, 1970), pp. 27–28.

ated with intimate disclosure to strangers is absent. As one expert has noted, "[the individual] must experience the group as a refuge wherein he is safe, wherein he can entertain new beliefs and experiment with new behavior without fear of reprisal." [4]

Most experiential groups, unlike traditional group therapy, are oriented toward the "here and now" rather than the past or future. The group process itself is the primary unit of analysis. For example, a long monologue by a group member about his past difficulties in marriage is apt to be interrupted by a demand for more immediacy, for greater concentration on reactions and feelings in the present. Disclosure of past experience is seen as relevant only when it relates to or explains current behavior in the group.

The emphasis on the present rather than the past and future is a fundamental tenet of Gestalt therapy, which has had much influence on the group movement. Fritz Perls,[5] founder of Gestalt therapy, asserted that civilized man spends so much time bemoaning his past and planning his future that he is unable to appreciate the present. The goal of much of Gestalt therapy, as well as much of the activity in experiential groups, is to help people live in the present and understand their current feelings.

WHY JOIN?

Self-disclosure and feedback from others are the two primary means by which experiential groups seek to promote change. Presumably, if an individual could discover for himself how both his behavior and his disclosures affected others, he might be more willing and able to change. Thus, experiential groups have been popular with business and government as a vehicle for improving human relations among employees and, hopefully, for improving productivity.

Experiential groups also have the potential to reduce racial and ethnic prejudice. Bringing together whites and blacks, Catholics,

---

[4] I. Yalom, *The Theory and Practice of Group Psychotherapy* (New York: Basic Books, 1970), p. 349.

[5] F. S. Perls, *Gestalt Therapy Verbatim* (Lafayette, Calif: Real People Press, 1969).

Protestants, and Jews, policemen and ghetto residents, may help
these people to understand how their customary behavior may
aggravate tensions. It is difficult for people to change deep-rooted
attitudes and behaviors, but as Kurt Lewin said, "This result occurs
when the facts become really *their* facts (as against other people's
facts). An individual will believe facts he himself has discovered in
the same way he believes in himself." [6]

Besides promoting self-insight, experiential groups purport to
sharpen interpersonal skills. Feedback from others may help
individuals learn how to make friends and get along with others. A
female newspaper reporter gave us this account of how a group
benefited her.

> I was really attacked by the group at one point. They said I was
> always acting superior. They said I had this air about me, that I
> thought I was always right and everyone who didn't agree was
> wrong and stupid. The people in the group said it made them angry.
> It really shook me up. I thought about the guys I work with. I've
> always wanted to be friends with them, but they seem to have this
> clique which they don't let me in. So I thought, "Well, maybe that's
> why." I tried acting differently, having more respect for their
> opinions, and it worked. They're much friendlier now, and one guy
> even remarked how much I had changed. But he never would have
> told me what he didn't like about me.

A potentially valuable contribution of groups is that they enable
people to rediscover their own feelings. A professor at our university
who tends to be very rational and intellectual told us:

> I had one experience in the group which was very moving, and I
> cried. I shocked myself—I hadn't cried since I was a kid. The group
> told me they thought I was finally being real, that I wasn't hiding
> behind my intellectual analysis of everything. The more I thought
> about it, the more I realized that I hadn't been in contact with my
> feelings. I mean, I didn't *know* what I was feeling—I never paid
> attention to them. So now I try to let myself react to things
> emotionally as well as intellectually.

In our interviews loneliness often emerged as a motive for joining,

---

[6] Quoted in A. Marrow, "Events Leading to the Establishment of the National
Training Laboratories," *Journal of Applied Behavioral Analysis,* 3 (1967), 144–50.

although this was never stated explicitly. A desire for intimacy and an opportunity to be accepted by others, even in the short, constricted time frame of the group, is a compelling motive. Carl Rogers has written eloquently on how the group can alleviate loneliness:

> . . . in an intensive group experience it is often possible for a person to peer within himself and see the loneliness of the real being who lives within himself inside his everyday shell or role. It is also possible for him to experience that loneliness fully, and find the experience accepted and respected by other members of the group. He can voice and bring into the open aspects of himself of which he has been ashamed or which he has felt were too private to reveal. To his surprise he finds that the members of the group feel far more warmly toward the real self than toward the outer front with which he has been facing the world. They are able to love and care for this real self, imperfect and struggling though it may be. . . . In that instant loneliness is dissolved, the person feels himself in real contact with another, and the estrangement which has been so much a part of his life vanishes.[7]

Experiential groups serve as "social oases"[8] in which conventional values are reversed. We are traditionally taught to wear a façade and to hide our real thoughts and feelings. The cost of taking off the mask can be rejection, embarrassment, humiliation, loss of friends, or perhaps even loss of job. In the group, in contrast, self-disclosure is valued and, hopefully, rewarded. Individuals are accepted when they express their feelings and thoughts openly. Persons may even be better liked when they present their real selves rather than when they hide their feelings.

Some individuals told us that they had learned a great deal about others and themselves from being in the group. In one's life, there are few persons whom one knows in any intimate way. Yet in a group experience one is allowed to see others on a very personal level, even though it is only for a brief time. The insights into others—their motivations, their feelings, their experiences—can be very useful and enriching, as well as providing a much-needed

---

[7] Rogers, *op. cit.*, p. 115.
[8] Yalom, *op. cit.*, p. 351.

perspective on one's own problems. A man in his mid-thirties told us:

> A man in my group got really upset and started crying when we talked about expressing real feelings. He told us that's how he lost his wife. One day he came home from work and she was gone. He said that he never told her that he loved her, that she really mattered to him. He just couldn't do it. And one day she left. It made me think about my own marriage, and my kids. I guess I expect them to know how much I care about them because I work hard to get them things. But I never told them, and I didn't even spend much time with them—I was too busy. After hearing that guy, I went home and told them all how I felt and told them I was going to cut down and spend more time with them. It wasn't easy, but I'm glad I did it.

Finally, an important goal of most experiential groups is to help the member grow psychologically, to facilitate his or her self-actualization. By increasing a person's self-awareness, his awareness of others, and his interpersonal skills, the group helps the individual make progress in fulfilling his potential as a human being, in becoming a more complete person.

Enthusiastic acceptance of experiential groups has led some employers to require their employees to participate. One person we interviewed, a middle-aged business executive who works for a large corporation, told us bluntly: "Why did I join? Simple—I was afraid I'd lose my job if I didn't! My company sent all its executives on this weekend marathon, and even though we were told we could refuse, no one did." Such coercion raises disturbing ethical questions regarding invasion of privacy. Most people, though, join groups voluntarily.

THE RISKS

For several years, controversy has surrounded the issue of the value of experiential groups. Many psychologists have heralded the virtues of "encountering," claiming that the group experience was a panacea for almost everything. It could reduce loneliness, increase interpersonal skills, foster psychological growth and self-actualization, and facilitate self-awareness. Carl Rogers, for example, calls the experiential group movement "one of the most rapidly growing social phenomena in the United States . . . perhaps the most significant social invention of the century." [9] Yet many critics have warned that there are pitfalls and problems associated with experiential groups, and that the consuming public should be aware of these problems. Such critics usually acknowledge that encountering is often a powerful technique, but they assert that the change produced in individuals is just as likely (or more likely) to be negative than positive.

One major problem of experiential groups is "reentry." After the experience of a weekend-long marathon group, a person returns to normal society, where the conventional norms of behavior and social discourse still apply. He has spent the weekend in an atmosphere where openness, feedback, and emotional expressiveness are encouraged; often, he will find the experience exhilarating and exciting. Back home, however, tact and emotional restraint are still the appropriate behaviors. He will be discouraged from engaging in too rapid self-disclosure or in too candid appraisals of his colleagues. If he attempts to act with his friends as he did in the group, he will likely encounter arguments or be ostracized or avoided for not conforming to the accepted rules of social discourse. In the movie *Bob and Carol and Ted and Alice* you may recall the scene where Carol, after her group experience, tries to encourage openness and self-disclosure from a waiter. The waiter becomes very uncomfortable and takes the first opportunity to leave her.

William Coulson, a prominent group leader considers reentry the first phase many individuals go through following encounter.

> First, having perhaps several days to bathe in the afterglow of the [encounter] experience, the individual wants to cause some of that glow in his own life. For a while, somewhat self-consciously, he begins to live by a new norm, in contrast to what was likely his old norm of caution. The new norm is one of revealingness. He wants to dare in his own life what he tried in the group and found valuable there.[10]

[9] C. R. Rogers, "Interpersonal Relationships: Year 2000," *Journal of Applied Behavioral Science*, 4 (1968), 265–80.

[10] W. R. Coulson, *Groups, Gimmicks, and Gurus* (New York: Harper & Row, 1972), pp. 90–91.

Unfortunately, the individuals with whom he "dares" to disclose personal feelings often feel threatened by this new behavior. Suddenly, he is providing feedback on how they appear to him, or he is telling them personal information that they consider too intimate and are not willing to reciprocate. Such deep self-disclosure may have the effect of making the recipient feel uncomfortable and pressured to respond in kind. Coulson has written of the reaction that such "open" behavior may elicit from others.

> Some college students of my acquaintance complained that their friends who had attended an encounter training program came back to the campus of a mind, evidently, to shock people. " 'Shit' seems to be their favorite word," one of the students said. "They're going around here bashing people with openness: 'Let me tell you how I see you,' uninvited—that sort of thing." [11]

According to Coulson, a "crisis" phase then occurs. The individual feels frustrated and dissatisfied as his friends resist his new behavior. This phase tends to be temporary and short, however, as the memory of the encounter fades and the reality of the outside world becomes more evident.

Reentry is a relatively minor problem for most experiential group participants. A more serious problem is that very few groups conduct any preliminary screening of their members. Thus, persons with histories of mental disorder and instability may join groups whose leaders are untrained to handle the emotional problems that the group may bring out in such persons. One psychologist and psychoanalyst who is a harsh critic of such groups has stated that "it is reprehensible to expose people unscreened for psychiatric illness or suicidal tendencies to an intensive and disruptive psychological process without protecting them with all possible skilled care and observation." [12] An unstable or emotionally disturbed person can be affected adversely by an experiential group. The person may not be capable of handling intensive, critical feedback from others. Rather than learning from such feedback, the person may become depressed and fall apart. One individual whom we interviewed told us of an incident in his group.

[11] *Ibid.,* p. 91.
[12] B. L. Maliver, *The Encounter Game* (New York: Stein and Day, 1973), p. 97.

There was a girl about twenty in our group. She was very shy and quiet; she hardly said anything at all. One guy started badgering her, asking her what her problems were, what she was hiding, and so on. Then some other fellows started on her, too. They said she came across as really uptight and cold, and they really disliked her. I kept waiting for the group leader to stop it, but he just listened. Soon she started to cry, and got really hysterical, and then she ran out. She never came back. I don't even think anyone ever checked on her to see if she was okay afterwards.

One goal of many experiential groups is, as Rogers terms it, "mask-cracking." Persons may be pressured to be "themselves," to strip away conventional façades and roles. Yet, such façades are often necessary if the individual is to continue functioning. Many people have constructed elaborate systems of defense mechanisms to block their own self-awareness and enable them to get along in the world. If these defenses are suddenly stripped away, the neurotic individual may not have the resources to cope with the experience. In such a sink-or-swim situation, some people may sink into a full-blown psychotic episode or a nervous breakdown.

One social psychologist who is involved in research on experiential groups has stressed the differences between constructive and destructive feedback.[13] The latter consists of labels—"John, you're a phony," or, "Mary, you're pushy and domineering." Such name calling makes a constructive response from the "victim" very difficult. Usually, he will either deny the allegation or, admitting it, feel inadequate and depressed. Constructive feedback takes the form of expressing feelings—"John, you make me feel angry and upset," or, "Mary, when you talk to me like that, I feel very helpless and submissive." Then the group can explore the reasons why the speaker elicits these feelings and can examine his actual behavior; in this way the group member will not feel that he is being attacked. It is the leader's responsibility to ensure that expression of feelings does not turn into a semantic game. Group members may preface their statements with catch phrases such as "I feel," without really changing their content. If a member says, "I feel that John is a

[13] E. Aronson, *The Social Animal* (San Francisco: W. H. Freeman, 1972), pp. 235–67.

phony," he is still expressing a judgment about John rather than a personal feeling that John elicits in him.

Insensitive group members, sometimes encouraged by an aggressive leader, may attack a member's behavior or personality, under the guise of constructive feedback. A person is especially apt to be attacked if he is perceived as violating the group's new norms of total honesty and self-disclosure. Very often, a group will be unable to accept reticence from any of its members. Here is the reaction of one group member to such an attitude.

> The last (group) meeting was particularly bitter for him since he was vigorously attacked for his passivity and uninvolvement. He recalls nervously picking at the carpet during the onslaught, he was criticized for this, and when he stopped picking at the carpet, was criticized for passivity and suggestibility. He was so shaken that he soon misinterpreted most comments directed at him, and perceived everything as criticism.[14]

Do Groups Work?

How common are psychological casualties in experiential groups? Is there a risk in participating? And is it reasonable to expect positive change from the group experience? Though there are hundreds of studies on group outcomes, most are flawed by such problems as inadequate control groups, ill-defined criteria of change, or lack of follow-up.

One problem with many outcome studies is excessive reliance on the self-reports of participants as indexes of change. Participants are asked to describe their own reactions to the group, either in open-ended form or in response to questionnaire items. Rogers speaks for many researchers in this field when he states: "This personal, phenomenological type of study . . . is far more valuable than the traditional 'hard-headed' empirical approach. This kind of study . . . actually gives the deepest insight into what the experience has meant." [15]

---

[14] M. A. Lieberman, I. D. Yalom, M. B. Miles, *Encounter Groups: First Facts* (New York: Basic Books, 1973), p. 184.

[15] Rogers, *Carl Rogers on Encounter Groups*, p. 133.

There is no doubt that such data are an important measure in studies of experiential group outcomes. Yet with no other corroborating data, self-reports are subject to bias. Psychotherapists have written about the "Hello-Goodbye" phenomenon, in which patients tend to magnify their problems at the start of therapy and to minimize them at the conclusion. In this way, a patient can justify the time, effort, and expense of therapy. He can also reassure his therapist in the process. For the patient to admit that therapy has failed, after the tremendous investment he has made, would be a painful experience indeed. Thus, the patient may distort reality to convince himself that his experience has been successful.

A similar process may take place in experiential groups. Here, as in psychotherapy, an individual has invested time, effort, and often money in the hope that he will find the group satisfying. He thus has a psychological interest in seeing the experience as positive. For this reason, self-report data alone are usually insufficient to prove that a group experience has been successful.

Lieberman, Yalom, and Miles have recently published the results of a very comprehensive study (cited in footnote 14). This study is noteworthy for the strength and rigor of its design. Eighteen different experiential groups with a total of 209 participants and 69 control subjects were studied. All subjects were college students who participated in the groups over the course of a semester for academic credit. The groups were led by sixteen experienced, professional group leaders. Their styles and orientation ranged widely from directive to nondirective, cognitive to emotional, and structured to nonstructured.

One important part of the study concerned the number of psychological casualties produced by the groups. A casualty was defined as

> an individual who, as a direct result of his experience in the encounter group became more psychologically distressed and/or employed more maladaptive mechanisms of defense; furthermore, this negative change is not a transient but an enduring one as judged eight months after the group experience.

The authors were particularly stringent in identifying an individual as a casualty. For example, a person who committed suicide midway through the project was *not* classified as a casualty because it appeared that his action was probably not a result of experiences in the group. One hundred and four persons were identified as potential casualties (by such criteria as peer evaluations, reporting a decrease in self-esteem, beginning psychotherapy, and so forth) and were interviewed. Ultimately, the authors labeled sixteen students, or 9.4 percent of the 170 who completed the study, as casualties. In most cases, the psychological damage that students incurred seemed to result from an attack on them by the leader, the group, or both, or from their unrealistic goals and expectations concerning the group. When these goals proved impossible to fulfill, feelings of inadequacy and hopelessness often occurred.

Whether a leader identified with a particular area or movement in psychology—such as Gestalt therapy, transactional analysis, or psychoanalysis—did not seem to affect the rate of casualties within a group. However, it would be erroneous to conclude that the behavior of the leaders was unimportant. Some groups had no casualties at all, and others had several. The particular leadership style within the groups appeared crucial in determining which groups would be the hardest hit. It was found that a high percentage of casualties occurred in groups whose leaders were aggressive and domineering, and sought emotional confrontations among members. These leaders were also highly self-revealing. In these groups, attacks on individual members were quite common. The casualty rate for members completing groups led by this type of leader was 14 percent. On the other hand, passive, laissez-faire leaders did not do very well either. Groups led by individuals who stayed in the background, neither stimulating the group nor offering it support, had the highest dropout rate (28 percent).

Leaders characterized as low on pressure and high on such dimensions as caring and affection produced the fewest casualties. The atmosphere in such groups tended to be more positive, less emotionally charged, and more cohesive. These results are consistent with the psychotherapy research that finds that a warm, supportive therapist is more apt to effect positive personality change than the therapist who is cold and distant. In the group, a warm leader can help structure a caring, accepting social environment in which destructive feedback is minimized.

In general, it appears that psychological injury as a result of group experience can be quite high, indeed unacceptably high, if the group is led by an aggressive, domineering leader interested in emotional expressiveness and confrontation. But a group with a passive leader unwilling to create an atmosphere of support or unable to stop the group from ganging up on a member can also generate casualties. But, one may ask, what about the positive features of the group experience? Do the benefits outweigh the liabilities?

Again, the comprehensive study by Lieberman, Yalom, and Miles appears to provide the best data. In assessing the amount of change (positive, neutral, or negative) shown by group members and control subjects, a number of criteria were used. These included self-report data, evaluations by group leaders, evaluations by significant others in the individual's life (relatives, friends, and colleagues), and a number of test measures. In general, the correspondence among all these criteria was low. Group leaders reported the most positive change, perceiving about 90 percent of the members as having experienced some positive change. Self-report data revealed that over 60 percent of those who completed the groups saw themselves as having benefited; this dropped to 46 percent when the subjects were interviewed six months later. At this time, 32 percent saw the experience as neutral and 21 percent saw it as negative. In contrast, friends and relatives were as apt to detect positive change in the control subjects as in the group members. According to this index, the group experience had little impact on the members.

To sort out these differences, Lieberman et al. developed a cumulative index, based on all the criteria including test measures. This index revealed that at the end of the group experience, about one third of the members changed positively (that is, they received positive benefits), a little over a third remained unchanged, and the remainder experienced some negative change or dropped out of the group. The 9.4 percent casualty rate came from this latter group; they consisted of extreme negative changers. Some of the types of change assessed (both positive and negative) were adequacy of interpersonal relationships (in terms of warmth, empathy, under-standing, and so on), sensitivity, adequacy of coping with problems, acceptance by others, self-esteem, positive conceptions of others, communication with others, and hours spent with close friends.

Some change in the percentages occurred during the six-month follow-up: about 75 percent of those who experienced positive change maintained the change; a similar percentage maintained their negative change six months later. Both the positive and the negative changes were significantly greater for group members than for controls.

As a result of their data, Lieberman et al. made this conclusion:

> . . . encounter groups show a modest positive impact, an impact much less than has been portrayed by their supporters and an impact substantially lower than the participants' views of their own change would lead one to assume.

DISCLOSING IN GROUPS

Self-disclosure might be described as the fuel that makes experiential groups run. Clearly, if no one in the group revealed their feelings and reactions, there would be no group. In the Leiberman et al. study, participants were asked to list the most important incidents that had happened in their groups; examples of self-disclosure were cited more often than any other single event. Seventy-five percent of these incidents involved self-disclosure by someone other than the reporting member. Perhaps the insight and perspective into one's own problems gained from hearing another's disclosure were responsible for this result.

Lieberman et al. suggest that the context in which disclosure occurred affected its impact. When self-disclosure was received with support and acceptance by the group, it tended to have a positive effect. Supporting this notion was the finding that the most productive disclosures occurred in the later sessions, when trust and support were more likely to be established. When these conditions are absent, the outcomes will be neutral or even negative. In general, the participants who benefited most from the group disclosed only under such conditions. The other members were not so selective. One casualty described by Lieberman et al. was a woman who revealed some intimate sexual problems . . . [and] received nothing in return except callous disinterest on the part of the group. . . .

She expressed considerable shame; it was difficult for her to take pride in herself after an experience she perceived as public humiliation. She took a risk, uncloseted her skeletons, discussed for example her feelings about her sexual relations with Black males, and was neither rewarded nor reassured by the group.

One reason why self-disclosure occurs so readily in experiential groups is that the participants are strangers. The group represents a kind of island, far away from the usual social contacts with friends, family, and co-workers. The participants are likely to meet one another for the first time in the group, and they are unlikely to meet one another in interactions outside the group. As we discussed in Chapter Four, disclosure is often easier to an anonymous stranger than to an acquaintance. The stranger moves on, posing little threat, and he is likely to be more objective. Yet, disclosure to a stranger can be harmful if rejection or ridicule ensues. The potential negative consequences are multiplied if the reaction comes from a whole group, not just a single individual. Such feedback can lead to shame and a sharp drop in self-esteem, especially if the disclosed material is important to the discloser.

When the participants in a group know one another, they often limit their disclosure and tend to avoid very intimate topics. Ralph Keyes recognized this problem in an experiential group he created at Prescott College in Arizona.

But mostly—and this was the issue on which I slipped up the most—this was a group of people living in a large community (of the college) and having to deal with each other over an extended period of time. I came in cold and the class was my main community at Prescott. I would be leaving shortly and risked little in taking chances to build a temporary community with this group of people. The class members had to deal with friends who resented our cliquishness. And they had to consider that anything they said to each other might be held against them in the future.[16]

[16] R. Keyes, *We, the Lonely People: Searching for Community* (New York: Harper & Row, 1973), p. 164.

To Join or Not to Join

Should one join an experiential group? This decision must be an individual one. Still, some guidelines can be given. First, a person should assess the goals he has set for himself regarding the group. If a person is very unhappy with himself and his relationships with others, and sees the group as a way to change all this, he should think twice before joining. Unrealistically high goals often lead to negative outcomes. Psychotherapy or counseling might be more productive for such a person. A person who is reasonably happy with himself, and who is generally stable psychologically but sees the experience as a chance to acquire some further interpersonal skills or self-insights, is more likely to benefit.

One should try to gain some information about the group leader and his training and style. In general, a warm, supportive leader who avoids pressuring members and does not encourage confrontation is likely to have few casualties and more positive change in his group.

As a participant, an individual should monitor his reactions to the group. If he still feels uncomfortable and alienated from the others after several sessions, or if he feels that he is not receiving any positive benefits, he should consider leaving the group. Making the decision to leave at this point is no index of failure; indeed, it may require courage and maturity to say, "I don't think the group is helping me."

Experiential groups are powerful agents for change. Further research along the lines of the Lieberman et al. study is needed to predict what conditions promote the most positive psychological growth for group participants.

COMMUNAL LIVING
Getting Back Together

A far more radical approach to achieving intimacy in our society is the communal movement. Communes are not a new idea (the nineteenth century saw the establishment of many communes in America, some quite successful), but the great number of communal experiments begun (and often disbanded) in the last ten years is unprecedented. Literally thousands of communes, most of them lasting less than two years, have sprung up during this time. Many groups have disbanded because of external or economic pressures. Others, however, have failed because the members simply could not learn to live together. Acrimony would increase, smoldering resentments would surface, members would begin leaving or planning to leave, and the commune would die. As we shall see, the way commune members handle and express (or suppress) their feelings about themselves and one another is an important factor in a commune's success.

Because of the great diversity among American communes, defining the term "commune" is not easy. Richard Fairfield, editor and publisher of *The New Utopian,* a journal devoted to the communal movement, defines a commune simply as "an arrangement of three or more persons among whom the primary bond is some form of sharing rather than blood or legal ties." [17] The "sharing" can range from common living areas, to shared economic activities, to an arrangement in which people form a "family" where all adults are equally responsible for child rearing and where monogamy no longer exists.

Characterizing American communes is difficult. Most are rural, but some are urban; some are very structured in their government and division of labor, but others are completely anarchistic; many (including some of the most successful) are based on a specific ideology, often religious in nature, but others have no underlying philosophy at all.

Yet some features are common to virtually all communes. Communalists share a dissatisfaction with the prevailing life styles of twentieth-century America. One sociologist has stated that "modern communal societies all maintain that the scale of society as currently organized is too large." [18] Most communalists reject the

[17] R. Fairfield, *Communes, USA: A Personal Tour* (Baltimore: Penguin, 1972), p. 1.
[18] R. E. Roberts, *The New Communes: Coming Together in America* (Englewood Cliffs, N.J.: Prentice-Hall, 1971), p. 12.

notion of status hierarchies and large, impersonal bureaucracies that inevitably accompany modern society. Most communalists also reject capitalist economics. They believe, in one form or another, in the Marxist maxim, "From each according to his abilities, to each according to his needs." Exceptions do exist, however. Many businessmen, for example, have joined urban communes because they can live more cheaply together than they can alone. Except for their share of the expenses, their income does not go into a communal treasury.

Most important, almost all communalists share the belief that a community should serve to reduce alienation and loneliness in its members. Kathleen Kinkade, a founding member of Twin Oaks, a successful commune in Virginia based on B. F. Skinner's utopian novel *Walden Two,* expressed this concept well:

> The communal idea is big enough to stimulate a lot of different dreams. . . . But commonest of all is the personal dream, the dream of no longer being lonely. Whatever else brings people to community, the hope of a compatible mate or a close, warm group of friends is usually just underneath the surface, and the success or failure of a person to be content with community often depends on his success or failure in finding love.[19]

It is too early to judge whether the modern communal movement will succeed. Certainly, most communes are short-lived. They face many problems: economic problems, disapproval and harassment from "straight" neighbors, and, most of all, internal conflicts—job assignments, jealousy, personality clashes, and debates about privacy versus openness. Though such problems can all be found in outside society, they are magnified by the pressures that arise when many different persons live together. Yet it is difficult to fault the communal ideals of friendship and intimacy. Even members of dissolved communes remark that they often miss the atmosphere of closeness, warmth, and community.

Certain factors do seem to correlate with communal success. One is structure: communes that lack structure or organization—everyone does his own thing in the name of freedom, and no norms for

---

[19] K. Kinkade, *A Walden Two Experiment: The First Five Years of Twin Oaks Community* (New York: Morrow, 1973), p. 2.

appropriate work behavior exist—often run into trouble. Where there are no defined work activities for members, the work is often not done at all, or is done by only a few. One commune member, Joyce Gardner, wrote bitterly about the "same small group doing all the work and taking care of the lazy transient people who only suck energy from the community and contribute almost nothing." [20]

HOW TO COPE: HONESTY OR DISCRETION?

Gardner's lament highlights the fact that interpersonal friction among communal members is a major cause of communal instability and collapse. In this context, the way communalists handle self-disclosure becomes critical. For example, should complete honesty among members be encouraged, or are tact and discretion more important? Should grievances against individuals be discussed candidly and face to face, or will such openness lead only to anger, bitterness, and the permanent exit of some members from the community?

Rosabeth Kanter has done some important correlational research on factors that are associated with successful communes. [21] One such factor is mutual criticism and/or confession. Kanter found that about half of the nineteenth-century communes in America that were successful (that is, that lasted over twenty-five years) practiced these techniques regularly, compared with less than a fourth of the unsuccessful communes.

Twin Oaks commune demonstrates a number of different ways in which grievances are disclosed. Kinkade has described some of them.

> What *can* one do about frustration with other people's unacceptable behavior? What are we supposed to do when we are just sick and tired of having the cows get out, or seeing the kitchen improperly cleaned—or for that matter, of hearing other people violate the gossip rule [a person should not criticize another behind his back]? We have tried several structures, all with some success, to handle legitimate criticism.

[20] Cited in Fairfield, *op. cit.*, p. 54.
[21] R. M. Kanter, *Commitment and Community: Communes and Utopias in Sociological Perspective* (Cambridge, Mass.: Harvard University Press, 1972).

The first was the appointment of a "Generalized Bastard." Brian thought of the idea, and we unanimously appointed him to the task. It was his job to relay unpleasant information. If I wanted to tell Quincy that he wasn't doing his share of the work, I was supposed to tell Brian, and he would tell Quincy without mentioning my name. Brian quickly found that he lacked the stomach for face-to-face encounters and reduced the system to note-writing. We lived with variations on this system for over three years. Now we have a box with a slot in the top called the "Bitch Box," where we can air our grievances if we lack the courage to go directly to the offender.[22]

Unfortunately, this solution was hardly ideal. Indeed, suspicion and hostility are almost inevitable results of such a roundabout system. A criticized member would undoubtedly begin to wonder who had criticized him and, if the criticism was especially severe, whom he could no longer trust. Before long, it would seem that the atmosphere within the commune might become very closed, cold, and untrusting.

Later, Twin Oaks adopted a face-to-face system modeled after the Oneidans' "mutual criticism." Though this method was probably healthier than the Generalized Bastard or the Bitch Box as a way of airing grievances and disclosing feelings, Kinkade notes that it too was not the perfect system:

The right not to attend [a mutual criticism meeting] is fundamental to Twin Oaks' sense of liberty. . . . For a long time . . . the people who would volunteer for criticism just weren't the people we were mad at. There wasn't much to say. Interest flagged.[23]

It is clear from this account that problems of interpersonal relationships and disclosure of feelings are critical in communes. Most communes do not exist very long unless these problems are handled with some degree of success. The solutions that communes have used to handle self-disclosure vary from a virtual absence of intimate disclosure to complete transparency. Sometimes, the consequences of maintaining interpersonal deception in a commune can be bizarre, as in this account of a commune:

The sex life of Heathcote is very weird. Everyone we have asked says [that he or she practices] monogamy here, except Alex, who claims

[22] Kinkade, *op. cit.*, pp. 151–52.
[23] *Ibid.*, p. 158.

to have fucked everyone. At dinner last night, they all outlined the sexual philosophy of the commune, saying the individual family is the core unit of life; husbands and wives, parents and children, traditionally alotted to one another. Said that living so closely with one another, the reverberations of one man or woman changing partners, leaving one or two others loose and therefore on the make, would be too violent and extreme for the place to tolerate. Surprisingly, it was the whole population of the commune telling this, nodding agreement, all in accord. In the three days I have been here it has been apparent that everybody is making it with everybody else and with all visitors. Just a while ago one guy came downstairs from his chick's room on the second floor, ran into his wife who was peeling potatoes in the kitchen, told her he was just back from a day in Baltimore. It would be a mistake to say there is any kind of sexual liberation here, because the enterprise is carried out with sneakiness and no honesty at all. In this way, Heathcote seems to resemble any suburban community. . . . They are all close to one another, relentlessly carelessly there in front of one another day after day, dinner after dinner, suspecting one another and holding grudges that last incredibly long times and bored with one another, and all these people are like a single obsessed brain. When they talk to me, it is obvious that each thinks of himself completely in terms of what the others think of him and how he relates to each one of the others.[24]

This vivid description highlights the dangers that can arise from a complete absence of disclosure within a commune. To a degree much greater than in the outside world, maintaining deceptions and façades in a commune can lead to stress, suspicion, hostility, and even paranoia.

Complete transparency is no panacea, however. Problems related to privacy—the need to be alone at times, both physically and psychologically—are usually solved in the outside world; they become more difficult in a commune. After a cross-country tour of many American communes, one observer wrote:

Everywhere, a screaming need for privacy, to be alone in a place called your own, one that was sacred and uncommunal. Everywhere, hassles and marathon encounter meetings that couldn't resolve

[24] E. Katz, *Armed Love* (New York: Holt, Rinehart and Winston, 1971).

questions like whether to leave the dogs in or out. . . . Everywhere, instability, transiency. Somebody was always splitting, rolling up his bag, packing his guitar and kissing good-bye—off again in search of the truly free, unhungup community.[25]

At another point, Houriet wrote:

At the commune, you couldn't change roles behind doors. Potentially, every minute was an encounter. There was no retreat. Your mumbling in your sleep could be overheard. Every little habit and personal idiosyncrasy was exposed.[26]

A dilemma faced by every commune is how persons living together can be open and transparent with one another but at the same time maintain some privacy and a sense of individual identity. One method used in some communes is for members to share the living areas but keep private or semiprivate sleeping quarters. In this way, one's need for solitude can be at least partially fulfilled.

For all their problems, communes represent one possible way of circumventing the loneliness that pervades modern America. Keith Melville and other contemporary critics have described the sterility of the modern suburb, where there are few, if any, places outside the home where people can meet. Melville notes that working-class neighborhoods still have their taverns, pool halls, and social clubs, but that these meeting places have no equivalents in middle-class suburbs. Suburbs are often only "bedroom communities": business and social lives are centered in the city, many miles away.

This arrangement is especially difficult for suburban youth, who lack the mobility and the money to take advantage of the city. Melville notes that "the suburban expectation is that almost all of one's important social and emotional needs can be satisfied by the immediate family." [27] It is no surprise, then, that many communalists are the offspring of suburban, middle-class parents. Having found little opportunity for genuine human contact in their suburban lives, many young people have turned to communes or to less radical solutions such as experiential groups.

[25] R. Houriet, *Getting Back Together* (New York: Coward, McCann & Geoghegan, 1971), p. xxxiv.

[26] *Ibid.*, p. 110.

[27] K. Melville, *Communes in the Counter-Culture: Origins, Theories, Styles of Life* (New York: Morrow, 1972), p. 175.

Both communes and groups appear to signal a general reaction against the alienation of modern life. Group participants have usually not rejected conventional life styles completely; when the group ends, they return to their families, their communities, and their jobs. Communalists, in contrast, have opted for a whole new way of living, one that is completely different from conventional life styles. Yet, though they differ so widely in substance and scope, groups and communes are both directed at bringing people together in a spirit of shared intimacy.

Whether these new innovations will achieve the goals they are seeking is uncertain. If they do not, it is safe to predict that even newer life styles and activities will emerge in the years to come, all seeking the elusive goals of community, solidarity, and intimacy.

eight

some concluding thoughts

Many facets of self-disclosure remain to be explored. More knowledge is needed, for example, about the role of disclosure processes in the development of new relationships. How does the disclosure process change over time? Do the topics for discussion change? Does reciprocity decrease with length of acquaintance? Does the importance of disclosure diminish as friendship and trust deepen?

The elusive relationship between disclosure patterns and mental health needs further study. One important topic, on which only a few studies exist, is the pattern of disclosure among the mentally ill, especially hospitalized psychiatric patients. Does unusual self-disclosure contribute to mental illness, or at least to the probability of its diagnosis? What patterns are indicative of probable improvement or cure? What really constitutes counternormative or "aberrant" self-disclosure?

Too much of our research has relied on college students as subjects because of their ready availability. Research on different groups of people must be conducted—for instance, the middle-aged and the elderly, and working-class people. Along this line, cross-cultural research—examining patterns of disclosure among different

138

societies—would be a fascinating avenue to pursue. Perhaps an understanding of a culture's norms governing self-disclosure will provide valuable clues about other features of that culture.

THE ETHICS OF DISCLOSURE RESEARCH

In his zeal to obtain information, the disclosure researcher must never forget the rights of his subjects. The situation may arise in which the individual's claim to privacy conflicts with the needs of behavioral research. In research it may frequently be necessary to record information about what people say and do in a manner that does not bias their responses. For example, tape-recording subjects' conversations without obtaining consent in advance enables the investigator to collect reliable and presumably honest data about subjects' self-disclosure. Unfortunately, such surreptitious recording raises serious ethical questions. The bugging of the Oval Office during the Nixon administration drove this point home for all Americans.

In conducting behavioral research, the investigator will occasionally infringe on the individual's privacy, or "right to be let alone," in Justice Brandeis's words.[1] Defined in absolute terms, the individual's right to privacy might imply that the researcher may never obtain personal information from a potential subject without advance consent. Given the possible problems in bias posed by obtaining advance consent from the subject, what solutions are available to the researcher?

A procedure that many researchers have adopted is to disguise the purposes of the study for which subjects have volunteered, collect the behavioral self-disclosure measures, and then ask the subjects' permission at the end of the experimental session to use their self-descriptions for data analyses. If such permission is not granted (an infrequent occurrence), the investigator can destroy the data on the spot. Further, the description that is used to recruit subjects need not misrepresent the study. The specific purpose may be veiled by describing it in general terms. For example, a study on

[1] Olmstead v. United States, 277 U.S. 438, 478 (1928).

self-disclosure between strangers may be presented as an experiment on "impression formation" or "the acquaintance process." These descriptions inform potential subjects in a general way about the areas of interest to be observed, but do not inform them in detail about the operations used to collect the data.

A key aspect in obtaining permission from subjects to use their data is confidentiality. Subjects' disclosures are identified by anonymous code numbers and are ultimately transformed into quantifiable form. Still, obtaining *post-hoc* consent from the subject is by no means an ideal solution. The data is already in hand when we ask the subjects for their permission to use it. An element of coercion may be involved in subjects' agreeing to our request to use their self-reports.

It would be desirable to investigate whether surreptitious recording is really necessary. To find out, a study is required in which some subjects are told in advance that their disclosures will be tape-recorded for analysis purposes and others are not. Then, the disclosures of both groups could be compared to see if they differ in any systematic way. If they did not, then future experiments could be more forthright in what subjects are told beforehand.

Most behavioral researchers believe that the importance of accumulating information justifies the occasional use of deception in their studies. Researchers, though, are deeply committed to their work and may inadvertently exaggerate their contribution. How do we balance legitimate scientific probing against threats to individual privacy? Two writers have suggested that a community consensus should decide if deception studies should be conducted.[2] Professional peers of the researcher, community leaders, and legal or other authorized representatives of those to be studied would evaluate the research. This suggestion has already been incorporated into research evaluation guidelines published by the U.S. Department of Health, Education, and Welfare.[3] A review committee—composed of individuals who are employed inside and outside

[2] O. M. Ruebhausen and O. G. Brim, Jr., "Privacy and Behavioral Research," *Columbia Law Review*, 65 (1965), 1184–1211.

[3] "HEW Regulations Restrict Biomedical, Behavioral Research," *APA Monitor*, 5 (1974), 4.

of the institution sponsoring the research—must evaluate and approve the project before HEW will support it.

There are no easy answers to the ethical issues we have discussed. Still, it is critical to make both researchers and potential subjects aware of the problems and sensitive to their responsibilities.

THE ROAD TO INTIMACY

Although much work remains to be done, there is still quite a bit that is known about self-disclosure. (Otherwise, we would not be writing this book.) We would like to conclude by summarizing some of the most important findings.

Perhaps the most common finding involves the reciprocal nature of self-disclosure. Disclosure by one person to another often leads to disclosure by the recipient. This occurs for several reasons, not the least being that intimate disclosure is one of the strongest indications one person can give to another that he is trusted. Since the discloser—by sharing personal information—has shown the recipient that he trusts him, the recipient assumes he can trust the discloser in return and so feels free to disclose himself.

This reciprocity norm is critical, it appears, in understanding the way friendships are formed. A person decides to entrust another with somewhat personal information. The other reciprocates. This is the beginning of trust and rapport between the two, and the next reciprocal exchange can be slightly more intimate. Assuming that nothing interferes with this spiraling process, the friendship between the two, based upon feelings of mutual affection, trust, and disclosure, will mature and deepen.

The reciprocity norm provides a good illustration of the relationship between neuroticism and appropriate self-disclosure. One of our studies (see Chapter Two for a detailed description) found that "normal" college students were much more likely to adhere to the reciprocity norm in their disclosures to another than were "neurotic" students. The results suggest that the relationship between neuroticism and self-disclosure is not a simple one, and that neurotics may have patterns of self-disclosure that are labeled as deviant or abnormal by most people.

Self-disclosure is risky. The initial discloser risks censure, ridicule, betrayal, and, perhaps worst of all, indifference from his confidant. The discloser who is reciprocating does not risk nearly as much; he knows that the other person now "owes" him at least the favor of listening. Yet the benefits of disclosing in appropriate contexts to suitable targets can be great. The joy of knowing another human being on a deep, intimate level, and of being known in return, is great; accomplishing this can add meaning and zest to life. However, achieving intimacy is not easy. The process is slow and gradual. Too rapid intimacy is fragile: it breaks down easily if one person discovers something negative or unacceptable about the other. On the other hand, an intimate relationship built upon a strong foundation of shared time, activities, and disclosures is difficult to destroy. In our opinion, the rewards of such relationships generously compensate for the time, effort, and risks involved.

index